Foil Fencing

The Techniques and Tactics of Modern Foil Fencing

Professor John 'Jes' Smith

British Academy of Fencing

Académie d'Armes Internationale

SUMMERSDALE

Summersdale Publishers Ltd
46 West Street
Chichester
West Sussex
PO19 1RP
UK

www.summersdale.com

Printed and bound in Great Britain

ISBN 1 84024 331 7

Cover image © Jake Martin/Getty Images

Acknowledgements

Every fencer learns from his master, and every master learns from his fencers.

So many personalities have, by their influence, unwittingly contributed to this text. Some have been first master or student and later friend, some have been constant companions or fleeting acquaintances. Some have even been rivals! Each has contributed an action, a concept, a thought or a remark that over time has fused with my appreciation of fencing to shape the way that I perceive the sport today.

Of the many coaches that I have known I would like to acknowledge my particular gratitude to two: Professor Roy Goodall and Professor Bela Imregi.

As for the many students with whom I have crossed blades, I thank them all.

Contents

Foreword

Fencing is currently undergoing a renaissance in Great Britain. Internationally we have had Junior European Champions at Men's Foil in 2001 and 2002, and our Men's Foil team won the European Team Bronze medal at the 2002 European Championships. Many fencing clubs are currently experiencing a real surge of interest, as fencing is a truly exciting and physically challenging but very safe sport. It is an ideal way to get rid of aggression and improve both personal discipline and health. It is also worth mentioning that the FIE (the international governing body) is looking to tighten up the rules and regulations concerning foil fencing to try to make it fairer, more logical and above all more comprehensible to a wider public.

Foil Fencing is an admirable book. In a clear and logical manner, Professor Jes Smith takes the reader from starting fencing to perfecting attacks and defences, and then on to more advanced tactics and techniques. At each stage he has clearly explained the techniques and added helpful diagrams and illustrations to clarify potentially confusing concepts. This book is an invaluable guide for beginner, intermediate or advanced fencers and is also an ideal syllabus for coaches to use.

Professor Jes Smith has a wide range of fencing and coaching experience and a real passion for the sport. I strongly recommend this book to fencing enthusiasts and beginners alike.

Keith A. Smith
President of the British Fencing Association

Introduction

Although fencing has variously been described as an art or science and many books on the subject dwell on the history of swordplay, fencing is a modern sport, requiring, like any other sport, commitment to physical endeavour, dedication to the necessary skills training, and the application of tactics. The three T's are the passport of today's fencer – Technique, Tactics and Timing. It is the unique combination of these three elements at any one moment that decides the success or failure of the fencer.

In this volume I have endeavoured to set out a practical guide that works progressively through the technical material of the sport, integrating offence and defence, basic and more advanced techniques, established practices and more innovative modern concepts. The work then brings this material together with a tactical summary that demonstrates how the concepts of offence, defence and counter-offence are interrelated.

I have deliberately omitted ancillary subjects such as fitness training, diet, administration and the rules, and focused exclusively on that one area that draws all of us to the sport of fencing – the use of the blade. It is my hope that anyone learning to fence can open this book at any page and find useful practical guidance on the use of the foil.

Having taught at schools, colleges and clubs in London for many years, I have met, trained and developed countless fencers. Regardless of their varied personalities, abilities and aspirations, they all had one common need: a source of reference that was both clear and comprehensive. This book is intended to satisfy that need and to enable any fencer, whether student, leisure fencer, competitor, junior coach or teacher, to see where any one stroke or tactic fits into the greater game, and to enhance their participation in this unique sport.

FOIL FENCING

Modern fencing, and in particular foil fencing, is far removed from the logic and practice of ancient swordplay. Today the fencer is safely clothed and protected, and often takes risks that his or her forebears would never have contemplated. Moreover these risks are not discouraged by the conventions of foil fencing (see Appendix A).

These conventions originate from the need to judge fencing as a sport rather than as true combat. In true combat a participant would avoid all risk of injury and endeavour to hit without being hit – a principle that is still valid today. However, in the modern sport the conclusion of a fencing phrase often sees both fencers receiving hits and then a judgement made as to which one, if any, scores. Basically the principle is that priority is given to the fencer who, at any one moment, has taken the initiative.

The result of these conventions is that a fencer, in some situations and contrary to natural instinct, learns to ignore the possibility of receiving a hit! So, not only is it necessary to master the technical material of the sport, but also to acquire and build new habits and responses. For this reason the novice recreational fencer should be prepared to spend some considerable time drilling a variety of sequences and appropriate reactions before participating in training bouts.

Once participating in lessons and bouts these conventions, from which the rules of fencing derive, become more apparent. As to the rules themselves, they are those of the Fédération Internationale d'Escrime (F.I.E.) and are subject to continual revision. During my time the rules regarding the fencing area ('piste') and its limits, the target, the weapons used, the number of hits, time duration, the permitted (or otherwise) use of hands and feet, and the formulae for both individual and team competitions have all been the subject of change. There is no reason to believe that they will ever remain static, and so the reader should, if intending to become a competitive fencer, be acquainted with the current regulations as published through the relevant national body.

With regards to the illustrations and exercises in this book, I have endeavoured to make them accessible to both left- and right-handed fencers. Many texts on fencing seem to work on the basis that everyone is right-handed and often include a short section entitled something like 'How to deal with the left-hander' delivered from a right-handed point of view. Here I have attempted to present the material such that it is equally accessible to all. However, if an illustration is not immediately clear then try viewing it in a mirror to obtain the reverse perspective.

The illustrative exercises following the presentation of a fencing stroke should work for two fencers of the same or opposite handedness. Where a particular stroke can be adapted to exploit an antagonist of the opposite handedness that is clearly shown in each section, rather than dealt with separately. In all the exercises the actions of Fencer B may be taken to be those of a teacher or coach, whilst those of Fencer A illustrate the stroke being developed. Additionally, the stroke illustrated is, in some cases, preceded with a preparatory action for context and realism; such preparatory actions may be omitted or modified.

Apart from the Game Practice sections, the exercises are drills in the use of the weapon, sword hand and feet. They demonstrate the technical material discussed and progress with the blade actions being presented, but I have also included three sets of Consolidation Exercises, bringing together previously covered topics so that strokes are not always practised in isolation.

A pedagogical note. You will find some exercises give Fencer B (the teacher) an either/or choice of action which then modifies the final action of Fencer A (the student). This enables the student to achieve flexibility in response to a given situation and to acquire fast, sure reactions. The fencer needs to be proficient at all elements of such an exercise before this concept of 'choice reaction' is introduced. Conversely, in other exercises, Fencer A has an either/or choice. In this instance, the student dictates how they will complete the exercise. This is important in developing the fencer's independence in decision-making.

FOIL FENCING

Those exercises that include a series of 'progressions' illustrate a technical or tactical development, and each progression needs to be practised several times before beginning the next, until the whole exercise is completed.

My aim and hope is to enhance the reader's participation regardless of their prior knowledge, and so each will probably approach this volume differently and take something different from it. The novice can work through the drills whilst reading ahead, the intermediate or club fencer might 'cherry pick' to add to their game, the competitive fencer might seek a new slant on tactics or timing, and the teacher could well be more interested in adapting the exercises. Whatever your approach, I hope you will both enjoy and benefit from this book.

Part 1: Starting Out

Principles

- To hit without being hit.

- To hit with the point.

- To hit the target – the torso at foil.

The guiding principle of all fencing is to hit without being hit. The hit at foil is made with the point and needs to be delivered accurately to the target, which is the torso – and that includes the flanks, shoulders and back as well as the more obvious chest and stomach areas. Every blade action and every tactic should be learnt and practised with this thought in mind. For every offensive action that the fencer learns, he or she needs to ask: When will I hit? Where will I hit? How will I hit? Will I be safe?

Many people taking up fencing for the first time have only the vaguest concept of the sport, and so do not have the wider context of a game into which they can apply their new abilities and knowledge. If this applies to you, then learn to observe the experienced fencers in your school, college or club. Identify the actions that you are learning and the tactics being used, how well (or otherwise) they are performed, and when they are performed. At first it will be difficult to follow two fencers in combat, but there is a simple trick to understanding – watch only one fencer. Observe how he or she manoeuvres, attacks and defends, and then the picture becomes clearer.

Although specific tactical advice is given later, the following brief summary is presented now in order that the new fencer can preview the use to which they can put their new-found blade skills. During the early months of learning, the repetition of mechanical actions to develop motor skills can cause the student to lose sight of the purpose to which their actions will be put, so whenever possible visualise those actions within the context of tactical application.

FOIL FENCING

Basic Tactics

- To attack from a covered ('engaged') blade position, denying the opponent the opportunity of hitting first.
- To attack during the opponent's preparatory action.
- To attack at the moment the opponent recovers from an action.
- To lure the opponent to attack into your defence.
- To false attack and then exploit your opponent's response ('second intention').

The Guard

The guard is the fundamental fencing position from which all blade, hand and foot actions are performed.

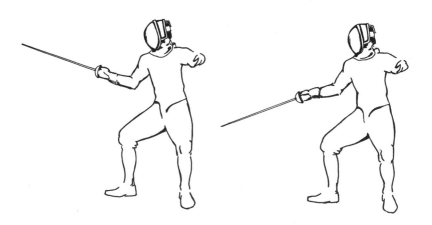

Fig. 1

The blade is held on the sword-arm side of the body, elbow lifted about a hand's span away from the waist and relaxed, as if you are about to shake hands with someone. The point may be raised (sixte position) or dropped (octave). (See Fig. 1.)

The leading toe and heel, together with the rear heel, should form a line to the opponent's leading foot; this is the fencing line. The knees and feet should be at right angles with each knee bent and above the corresponding foot. The feet should be a minimum of two foot-lengths apart. The hips and shoulders form a natural angle of about thirty degrees to the fencing line. Avoid turning the body either squarely or obliquely to the opponent as this exposes unnecessary target area whilst adversely exaggerating the blade position. The rear arm is held loose to the side and is raised for balance and safety; the shoulders remain level and relaxed.

To advance in this position, lead with the front foot. Raise the toe and then advance the foot a short distance, landing with a heel-toe action. The rear foot then follows by being lifted and replaced forward without dragging.

To retire, place the rear foot back a short distance as the front toe lifts. The front foot, pushing off from the heel, is then retired an equal distance. When stepping, the centre of gravity always remains between the feet and is never permitted to shift over either foot, and importantly, the fencing line is maintained to ensure the correct alignment with the opponent at all times. Further foot actions are dealt with later, and development exercises are found in Appendix B.

The Grip

The grip refers to the manner in which the foil is held and does not imply that the weapon is held strongly or rigidly in one fixed position. In fact, correctly held, the weapon is balanced in the hand, the fingers relaxed and the handle mobile.

There are two types of foil handle: French and orthopaedic or pistol grip. (See Fig. 2.) Whichever handle is used the grip is the same. The thumb and forefinger (the 'manipulators') control the blade direction whilst the other fingers (the 'aids') assist.

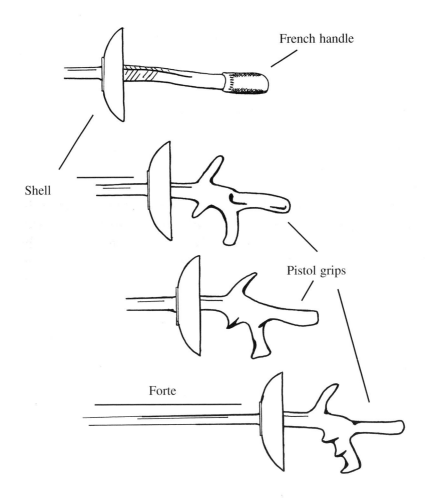

French handle

Shell

Pistol grips

Forte

Fig. 2

The weapon is held about half a centimetre inside the shell between the ball of the thumb, which rests on top of the handle, and the second phalange of the forefinger which is directly opposed. There should be no noticeable gap between the thumb and the forefinger. The remaining fingertips lie along the side of the handle. (See Fig. 3a.) With the orthopaedic grip, the first two fingers are placed ahead of the forward, trigger-like projection on the underside of the handle. The upper projection nestles between the thumb and forefinger.

As there are a number of equipment manufacturers producing handles in different styles and sizes, when selecting a weapon choose one that permits the weapon to be held comfortably, with the point of balance of the weapon just forward of the guard. Our hands are not all formed according to the manufacturer's specifications and in some instances it may be necessary to modify orthopaedic handles to individual requirements. The length of the handle between the shell and the projections may have to be shortened or lengthened in order to bring the thumb and forefinger into the correct position. Additionally the upper projection may have to be modified to permit the thumb to lie along the top of the handle. As handles are made of either plastic or aluminium this is not difficult. The weapon can be disassembled by releasing the locking nut in the base of the handle, and most clubs have an armourer who can give guidance or assistance.

With both the French and orthopaedic handle there should be some degree of angle between the blade and the handle. The handle should be offset down and inwards. This ensures that the line of the blade and the direction of the point is a continuation of the line of the thumb and can be accurately and naturally directed from the hand.

The hand is rotated so that the thumb is turned slightly outwards from the upright with the knuckles underneath. Maintain a loose wrist, flexed slightly inwards but outside the line of the elbow, which should point down and not to the side.

A push-pull action between the thumb and forefinger will cause the point to rise and fall. Similarly, rotating them will cause the point to describe circles. The action of the thumb and forefinger is assisted by the other fingers, which open and close the handle against the palm but always retain contact with the handle.

Fig. 3a

Fig. 3b

Fig. 3c

The forefinger should not be extended (see Fig. 3b) nor should the other three fingers be permitted to wrap around or take control of the handle. (See Fig. 3c.) Although these actions may appear to ease the workload of the thumb and forefinger, they will inhibit the development of the hand. Consequently blade manipulation will suffer as it will lack the direction and accuracy that only the thumb and forefinger can give.

A simple exercise for the hand is to hold the foil by the blade with the handle on the ground, then manipulate the thumb and forefinger in coordination with the other fingers to gradually lift the foil by passing the blade through the hand. The manipulation of the forefinger and thumb may also be practised by placing two small coins between the second phalange and the ball of the thumb, and then rubbing the coins forwards and backwards, sideways and in circles and semicircles in both directions.

Blade Manipulation

Delivering a Hit

To deliver the point to the target requires subtle and progressive coordination in the use of the hand and arm. From the sixte position manipulate the handle so that the blade rises and falls, and then on a falling action of the blade allow the arm to rise and lengthen. This lift and propulsion should come from the triceps muscle located under the arm between the elbow and armpit. The sensation should be that of the elbow being lifted as if on an elevator. The muscles of the shoulder are not used. The hand should finish at a level slightly higher than that of the opponent's shoulder and be outside the line of the mask (see Fig. 4a) with the point striking the target just before this final extension is achieved.

Delivered in this manner the fencer can develop full and efficient use of their reach and, as the hand is rising at the moment of striking, deliver the hit safely and without undue brutality when first practising.

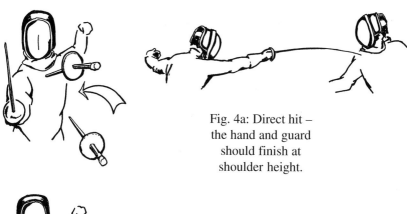

Fig. 4a: Direct hit –
the hand and guard
should finish at
shoulder height.

Fig. 4b: Angulation – greater
height or direction to the side
can be used to achieve
angulation.

The action can be exaggerated to create greater angulation if needed. (See Fig. 4b.)

When practising the conclusion of the hit, do not place the sword hand in front of your face. This will have three unwanted effects: it will (1) obscure the blade and target; (2) misalign the weapon on its flight to the target; and (3) shorten your reach. Remember to conclude the action as shown above.

You may wish to practise the hit in 'opposition', that is, the stroke finishes in an alignment corresponding to the opposite shoulder and is used to close out the possibility of a counter-thrust by the opponent. (See Fig. 5.)

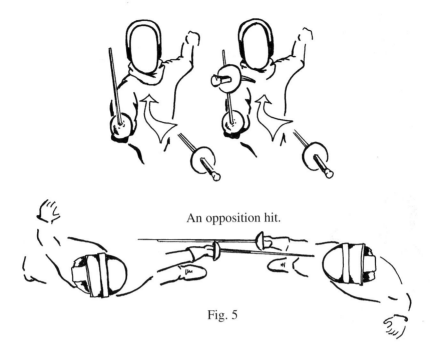

An opposition hit.

Fig. 5

Practise delivering the hit with a step forward. Starting from sixte or octave, the action of the fingers precedes the impetus from the triceps, which is followed by the step. The total action is co-ordinated such that the point lands on the target as the step is completed. Additionally, to ensure that the hand rises correctly and finishes at the proper height, practise the hit while advancing from a guard of sixte and delivering the hit over an obstacle such as a mask or foil blade held between the fencers (as in Fig. 6). Similarly angulated hits can be practised by hitting around the side of an obstacle, directing the arm extension to the side whilst the fingers and hand form the necessary angle to direct the point to the target.

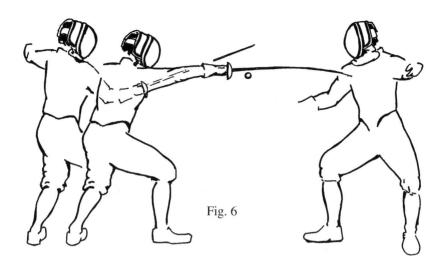

Fig. 6

Practise delivering a hit from sixte and stepping back from the target to a guard of sixte or quarte. The point should travel in an arc-like trajectory, arriving at the target with more the character of a thrown dart than a punch. Balance should be maintained throughout. A common error with the novice fencer is to push the hit forward either during or after the delivery to the target. Such a push unbalances the fencer and compromises their ability to perform subsequent actions. Remember that in combat it is necessary to hit not only whilst advancing, but also while retiring or recovering from an attack. If the fencer pushes forward with the shoulder or body whilst retiring with the feet, contrary forces are at work; therefore the hit must be learnt in a manner that allows the fencer to maintain equilibrium.

Having become proficient at hitting at full reach, the fencer may then consider other methods of delivering the point to the target (see Part 5: Additional Combat Skills).

Transports

There are four guards for the novice fencer to master: sixte and octave on the sword-arm side, and quarte and septime on the opposite side. Note that we do not refer to 'left' and 'right', but that all blade positions are common to both left-handed and right-handed fencers. (See Fig. 7a.)

To practise the controlled movements necessary to change position, have a partner place their blade *horizontally* with the tip just resting on your shell. Then use your blade to manoeuvre the tip to different locations as illustrated. (See Fig. 7b.)

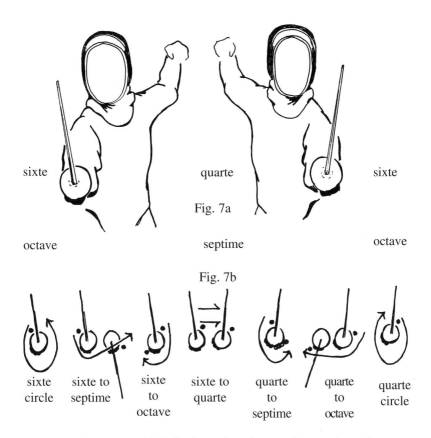

sixte   quarte   sixte

Fig. 7a

octave   septime   octave

Fig. 7b

sixte circle | sixte to septime | sixte to octave | sixte to quarte | quarte to septime | quarte to octave | quarte circle

Place the partner's blade horizontal on the guard at • and practise manipulating to the various positions.

(Illustrated for right-handed fencer.)

When comfortable with these actions, conclude them with a hit to the target. In addition, practise the sequences in Figure 7c, concluding with a hit.

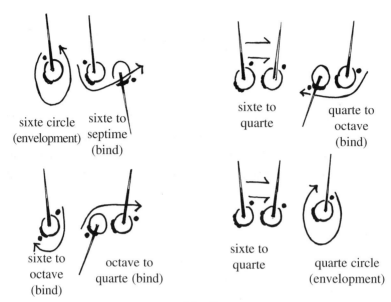

sixte circle (envelopment)   sixte to septime (bind)

sixte to quarte   quarte to octave (bind)

sixte to octave (bind)   octave to quarte (bind)

sixte to quarte   quarte circle (envelopment)

Fig. 7c

Linked blade actions. Place the partner's blade horizontal on the guard at • and practise the successive blade manipulations shown.

(Illustrated for right-handed fencer.)

The Blade for Preparation, Offence and Defence

Control of the blade both in and between the four basic positions is essential for attack and defence. It is entirely possible to score a direct hit on an opponent by relying purely on timing and without any blade preparation. However, the novice fencer is best advised to prepare his or her attack with preliminary actions on the opponent's blade. These can take the form of 'engagements'.

When two fencers stand facing each other, they usually adopt a guard in either sixte or octave without contact of blades ('absence of blades'). This also means that each fencer is exposed to the possibility of attack by the other. In launching an attack there exists the distinct possibility that the opponent may simultaneously attack (probably in panic), and thus no one scores and injury may result.

By the simple expedient of placing your blade on the opponent's ('engagement') you are 'covered' and deny your opponent the opportunity of an immediate attack. (See Fig. 8.) Because of your positional advantage you may then launch an attack. If your opponent extends to hit, they will have commenced after your attack and be 'out of time', with your initial attack having priority. From sixte or quarte, if the hand is maintained in the line of the engagement then the attack will be delivered in opposition (see Fig. 5, page 21) and will be entirely safe.

Engagements commencing from sixte to …

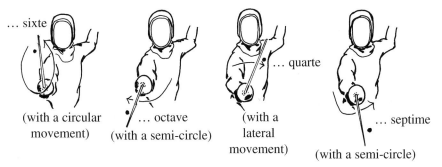

… sixte

… quarte

(with a circular movement)

… octave
(with a semi-circle)

(with a lateral movement)

… septime

(with a semi-circle)

Fig. 8

The blade is divided into three sections. The first thirty centimetres or so from the point is the most flexible part of the blade and is known as the 'foible', whilst the rigid base of the blade nearest the guard is the 'forte'. The area between constitutes the middle of the blade.

To form an engagement, use the upper part of the blade towards the foible to make contact. When engaging in quarte it is not necessary to carry the hand fully across the body. Allow it to rotate about thirty degrees whilst it is carried across and forward about ten centimetres. When engaging in sixte the hand must finish in the basic guard with the blade directed slightly outwards so that the opponent is denied any direct hit to the sword arm.

Practise the hit with a step forward preceded by an engagement in one of the four lines. Check that the feet do not move until after the release of the blade so that the initiation of the hit precedes the footwork. Practise the formation of an engagement during the latter half of a step forward and follow this with a hit delivered with a second step forward.

Whereas the middle and foible of the blade are used to form engagements, when a defensive action is required, contact is made using the forte, and for prises de fer the forte and possibly the shell of the weapon is used. Figure 9 illustrates these actions initiated from the sixte guard.

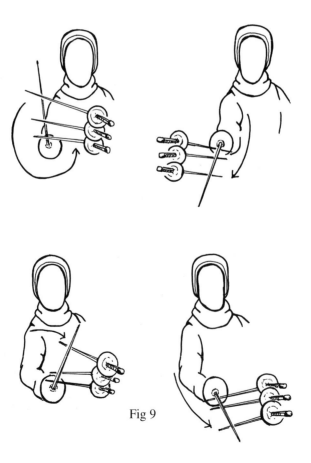

Fig 9

The Lunge

Offensive actions with a step forward are useful for the practice and learning of new blade actions as they enable the fencer to develop balance and moderate his or her speed whilst learning new techniques. Such actions delivered with speed are also applicable to combat, but the classic attack is the lunge. (See Fig. 10.)

Again the commencement of the offensive blade action should precede any footwork. Having initiated a hitting action from the fingers and triceps, the front toe should leave the ground (as in the commencement of the step) but should continue further by allowing the leading leg to extend fully. Maintaining the centre of gravity between the feet, the rear leg is thrust straight (rear foot remaining flat) just before the front heel lands. As with a step the front foot lands heel-toe.

The development of the lunge.

Fig. 10

Towards the end of the lunge the rear arm is extended to add the final impetus and maintain balance. It should be extended from the elbow with the palm facing up. Excessive use of the rear shoulder for this action will twist the body and misdirect the sword arm. Similarly if the palm finishes face down it will cause the rear shoulder to turn inwards, distorting the natural angle of the body and causing the fencer's weight to fall forward. The hit should arrive a fraction of a second ahead of the front heel landing.

During the lunge the fencer's body sinks in relation to the on-guard position and the opponent. Therefore it is necessary to develop the habit of permitting the sword hand to rise throughout the lunge and, in practising, to check that it finishes at shoulder height. (See Fig. 4a.)

In the final position of the lunge the leading knee rests above the leading foot and the front thigh is parallel to the ground. In this position the fencer is balanced and can perform further blade actions if necessary. If the foot finishes ahead of the knee, then the fencer has 'over-lunged', risking strain and making it impossible to recover. If the knee finishes ahead of the leading foot, then the fencer has not extended the leading leg sufficiently during the development of the lunge; the result is that the body weight rests forward of the knee, causing strain to the knee and difficulty with any recovery to guard.

To recover from the lunge: classically the rear knee bends and the muscle contraction of the rear leg pulls the fencer back as the front heel pushes off. With a sitting action, the fencer returns to guard, relaxing the sword arm into sixte or quarte. The front foot returns with the heel being placed first and then finally the front toe. Less strenuous is to recover forward (assuming that the opponent has given ground) by bringing the rear foot forward and rising slightly.

To develop a good appreciation of the lunge and the mechanics of lunging, start in the final lunge position, form a recovery and then re-lunge. This also assists in maintaining the rear foot flat on the floor. Although competitive fencers may roll or slide the rear foot as a result of a dynamic attack, the novice fencer is encouraged to keep the rear foot flat for stability, balance and to develop an appreciation of reach and distance.

The successive actions of the lunge (the development) can take several cadences. They can be performed very fast and dynamically as an explosive action and cover a slightly reduced distance. Alternatively the development may be such that it starts at a gentle pace and then accelerates towards the conclusion of a slightly elongated lunge. Care must be taken that the centre of gravity is maintained throughout, especially in the latter type of lunge. If the body is pushed forward over the leading leg then the transfer of weight forward will cause the front foot to land prematurely and shorten and unbalance the lunge.

In order to become familiar with both correct balance and delayed acceleration, the lunge can be practised in two phases, separated by momentarily resting the leading heel on the ground midway through the lunge. This action itself can become a third cadence in developing an attack. The form of lunge applied at any one time is dependent on the distance to the opponent and the stroke being employed. For example, an explosive lunge may follow a beat on the opposing blade, an accelerating lunge could accompany a compound attack, and a lunge that is paused might be used with 'broken time'.

Practise the hit delivered by step and by lunge, then practise engagements (with or without a step) followed by lunges from all four lines. Remember to adjust the distance appropriate to the footwork being used and include a variety of cadences with the lunge.

To practise or check the correct movement of the leading foot at the commencement of the lunges, place a coin under the heel, raise the toe and propel the coin with the heel. To prevent your body weight moving forward at the beginning of a lunging exercise, start on guard with the front toe raised to prevent unnecessary forward transfer of the centre of gravity.

Fencing Distance

This is defined as the lunging distance needed in order to reach the target. Conventionally it is the minimum distance maintained by fencers as they manoeuvre and thus is the normal distance during the individual lesson or pairs practice. It is essential that the fencer develops an appreciation of distance and that awareness of the fencing distance becomes as tangible as the touch of a blade. However, although this distance may be the normal distance for training, it is not always the most appropriate. When acquiring new blade skills it is counterproductive and unnecessarily fatiguing for them to be accompanied by repetitive lunging, the quality and speed of which would be diminished. In this case a shorter distance is appropriate, and once the blade skills have developed they can be integrated with the lunge.

Conversely, fencers who consistently maintain fencing distance during a bout will find themselves at a disadvantage. They risk surrendering control of the distance by following the opponent, thus giving the initiative to the opponent. Rather, the realistic distance for fencing is slightly longer than the classic fencing distance; coming into fencing distance should be a conscious act. If a fencer has no expectation of attack or of the opponent's action, he or she should not enter fencing distance other than to explore, provoke or tease and then retire. This means that, in developing the fencer, this longer distance (with accompanying footwork) should be employed for competitive and tactical training, thus developing the initiative that a fencer needs. Fencing distance then is that used for the practice and drilling of known actions and reactions and is modified for learning and competitive situations.

Changes of Engagement

When a fencer's blade is engaged by the opponent then, clearly, the opponent has a positional advantage in that he or she may more readily launch a hit. To counter this, either give a slight pressure against the opposing blade, moving it laterally so that you become 'covered' or, by dipping the point under the opposing blade, come up on the inside to form an engagement to your advantage.

Figure 11 shows a left-handed fencer freeing their blade from the opponent's engagement and 'changing the engagement' so that they are covered in their sixte line.

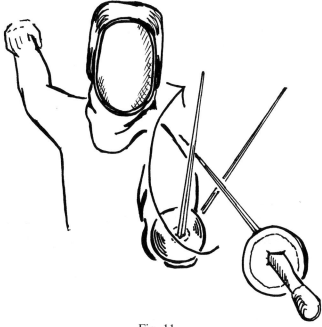

Fig. 11

- Practise a series of three or four changes of engagement with a partner. Finish by stepping out of distance and forming a guard.
- Practise stepping forward with engagement/changes of engagement whilst a partner steps back with changes of engagement.
- Practise a series of two or three changes of engagement and conclude by hitting with a step or lunge.
- Practise stepping forward with an engagement, permit the partner's change of engagement and then change the engagement once more before attacking with a lunge.

It is important that on each change of engagement the opponent's blade is dislodged and that the fencer gains a covered position.

Exercises

Fencer A: step with an engagement in quarte.
Fencer B: circular change of engagement.
Fencer A: circular quarte change of engagement and attack.

★

Fencer A: step with an engagement in octave.
Fencer B: give pressure.
Fencer A: circular septime change of engagement and attack.

It is important to develop the sense of touch through the blade ('sentiment du fer'), to feel and distinguish between the pressure or detachment of the opponent's blade, in order to respond appropriately. Try practising with your eyes closed!

By practising blade manipulations and guards the fencer should develop a feel as to the limit of these actions. That is, the fencer should not move any further from their guard than is necessary to remain covered. Some fencers will, from panic or heavy-handedness, move their blade excessively to one side. The result is that they will (1) expose more target than is expedient, and (2) need more distance and time to perform a subsequent action, giving the advantage to a neater, more time-efficient opponent.

When engaging a blade, complete the action at the point where your target is covered and do not pursue the opponent's blade should it continue in the direction that you have sought. Rather, permit it to continue moving out of line and direct your attention to the attack instead.

Against the opponent's engagement or pressure it is easy for the novice fencer to overreact when changing the engagement by returning the pressure, instinctively trying to push away the threat. Developing a circular change of engagement as a response to such stimuli is physically less demanding and permits the fencer to remain calm and in control.

Game Practice

With a partner, starting outside lunging distance, play a game where either fencer may advance into distance with a guard or engagement. The two fencers then attempt to seek an advantageous engagement so that they are 'covered' and the opponent is not. After a few mutual changes of engagement either fencer may break off by retreating out of distance. Additionally each fencer should strive to seek a positional advantage so they could launch an attack. However, at this stage, simply launch the extension (to which the other fencer should respond by stepping back and not automatically parrying).

The objectives are: (1) to develop blade control, 'sentiment du fer' and spatial awareness; (2) to find the moments from which an attack can be launched and to realise the time available; (3) to build the ability to move safely into and out of distance; (4) to observe your opponent's habits and level of skill; (5) to discover how your opponent responds to threats, that is, your extension.

Repeat the previous game practice steps, but do not always change the engagement. Instead, occasionally release the blade (e.g., on the opponent's engagement of sixte do not change to your line of sixte or quarte but free the blade to octave or septime). Does the opponent overreact to pursue your blade, in which case they may be vulnerable to an attack, or do they instinctively want to attack, in which case they will be vulnerable to a premeditated defence?

Defence: Parry and Riposte

The basic form of defence with the blade is the parry. The parry requires that the forte of the blade opposes the foible of the attacking blade in order to deflect it. Little effort is required because of the greater strength and leverage afforded by the forte at the base of the blade.

Parries are conventionally classified as:
1) simple: lateral actions, e.g. from sixte to quarte.
2) circular: starting and finishing in the same guard, e.g. circular sixte or circular quarte.
3) semicircular: moving from high to low, or vice versa. This category may be subdivided into parries which are formed on the same side (e.g. from sixte to octave), and those which move diagonally and finish on the opposite side (e.g. from octave to quarte).

To develop well-executed, controlled parries, it is first necessary to master transporting the blade to a final line, then the engagement in that line, and finally the parry against a feint or thrust in that line.

The final position of a parry will be dependent on the type of attack and the final distance between the two fencers. Basically the closer the fencers finish, the further the final parry will need to be carried to ensure that the target is completely closed. A quarte parry, for example, may have to be carried somewhat wider and lower, or a septime parry wider and higher than illustrated. Conversely, the earlier a parry is taken (and therefore at a greater distance from the target being protected) the shallower and more advanced is the position of the defending hand. The quality of the parry may also change with a more beat-like action being used for advanced hand positions whilst deeper parries rely more on the quality of opposition. Additionally, the more advanced parries may also employ the middle of the blade rather than the forte in order to deflect the attacking blade.

For the novice fencer the position of the parry should be as with the corresponding guard or slightly advanced – the natural tendency to withdraw the hand defensively should be avoided. The previous remarks about limiting and controlling the actions of engagement apply equally to parries.

A parry will be formed either as an instinctive reaction to a threat or attack, or as a premeditated tactical response to a known attack. In the former case the new fencer is likely to overreact, and it is better to first develop the technical skills and tactical application of the parry before progressing to reactions to feints and deceptions (see also Part 5, 'Defence: Parries – Reaction, Premeditation and Inducement').

Exercises

Fencer A: on guard in sixte.
Fencer B: place blade horizontally on the outside, upper part of Fencer A's shell.
Fencer A: describe a complete circle to finish covered in sixte ('sixte envelopment').

★

Fencer B: engage Fencer A's foible on the inside.
Fencer A: describe a complete circle (sixte change of engagement).

★

Fencer B: extend with a deep feint inside Fencer A's shell.
Fencer A: describe a complete circle to deflect the attacking blade.

Note that in the defensive action above, Fencer A's point should describe a large circle to ensure that the attacking blade is met with the forte. Too shallow a blade action will cause the blades to meet at their mid-points, thus depriving

---

the defender of the advantage of leverage. The defender's hand may remain in place or describe a small ellipse, and the parry takes the character of opposition.

★

Fencer A: on guard in sixte.
Fencer B: place the blade horizontally on the inside, upper part of Fencer A's shell.
Fencer A: transport the blade to octave with a semicircular action.

★

Fencer B: lower blade to octave.
Fencer A: form an engagement in octave.

★

Fencer B: extend with a deep feint below Fencer A's shell.
Fencer A: take a semicircular parry of octave, deflecting the threatening blade with opposition of forte to foible.

The exercises above should be practised with the following footwork: (1) in place; (2) with a step forward with the blade action during the first phase of the step or the conclusion of the step; (3) with a step back with the blade action during the first phase of the step or the conclusion of the step.

A fencer is in the most advantageous and dominant position when he or she has just successfully completed a parry. They have the initiative and the right to 'riposte' (see Fig. 12), the failed attacker has lost the advantage, is probably panicking and is within hitting distance. From the parry take a moment to pause and observe the failed attacker then calmly place the riposte either direct, or with angulation or opposition. The action of riposting should commence from the fingers, and the fencer should avoid any undue haste that may cause the arm or feet to precede the control of the point.

The riposte

Fig. 12

Exercises

Fencer A: step forward with an engagement in quarte.
Fencer B: change engagement and attack with a step or lunge.
Fencer A: parry with circular quarte and riposte direct or in opposition.

★

Fencer A: engage in sixte.
Fencer B: change engagement.
Fencer A: lower point to octave.
Fencer B: attack with step or lunge.
Fencer A: parry with sixte or quarte, riposte and step back.

At the completion of the riposte the fencer should relax the sword arm and step back into on guard. The final guard may be indicated by a partner or coach with their blade. Later such an indication can be given as a feint thrust, so that the fencer completes a parry-riposte exercise with a further parry. This in turn may be followed by a further riposte (second counter-riposte).

Exercises

Fencer A: engage sixte.
Fencer B: disengage thrust with a step (or three-quarter lunge).
Fencer A: parry quarte, riposte and step back to sixte.
Fencer B: with the blade, indicate a final position of sixte, quarte or octave for Fencer A.

★

Fencer B: continuously advance, threatening the upper target at quarte and sixte alternatively.
Fencer A: retire with a succession of quarte-riposte and sixte-riposte.

★

Fencer B: continuously advance, threatening the upper target at quarte and sixte randomly.
Fencer A: retire with a succession of quarte-riposte and sixte-riposte as appropriate.

*

Fencer B: advance with a feint high, feint low, feint high.
Fencer A: retire with quarte-riposte, octave-riposte, sixte-riposte.

Because of the conventions of foil fencing it is important that a fencer does not automatically continue to hit if they fail with a riposte as the 'right of way' will pass to the successful defender. Rather, the fencer first needs to nullify any threat by the opponent in order to regain their turn. A succession of parries and ripostes helps to develop this appreciation. For more realism, in the last exercise above, Fencer B can parry the first or second (or both) of Fencer A's ripostes.

Although the parry is classified as a defensive action, that does not mean that the fencer has to take a purely defensive role in employing it. Additionally fencers should avoid the indiscriminate parrying of threats and develop the use of the parry to take the initiative from the attacker. This can be achieved by using footwork and distance control as a means of defence.

Exercises

Fencer A/B: engage in the low lines of septime/octave.
Fencer B: advance or retire one or two steps.
Fencer A: maintain distance.
Fencer B: periodically threaten Fencer A with an extended arm and blade.
Fencer A: do not respond.

Fencer B: periodically threaten Fencer A and develop a lunge.

Fencer A: parry as late as possible and step back (with or without a riposte).

*

Fencer A/B: engage in the low lines of septime/octave.

Fencer B: advance or retire one or two steps.

Fencer A: maintain distance.

Fencer B: periodically threaten Fencer A with an extended arm and blade.

Fencer A: do not respond.

Fencer B: periodically threaten Fencer A and develop a lunge.

Fencer A: do not parry but try to retire using distance as a defence.

*

Fencer A/B: engage in the low lines of septime/octave.

Fencer B: advance or retire one or two steps.

Fencer A: maintain distance.

Fencer B: periodically threaten Fencer A with an extended arm and blade.

Fencer A: do not respond.

Fencer B: periodically threaten Fencer A and develop a lunge.

Fencer A: either retire using distance as a defence or parry and riposte.

*

Fencer A/B: on guard in sixte with absence of blades.

Fencer B: continually advance and retire one step.

Fencer A: maintain distance.

Fencer B: periodically threaten Fencer A with an extended arm and blade.

Fencer A: do not respond.

Fencer B: attack with lunge or step-lunge at will.

Fencer A: try to defend with distance, or parry late, or if the step-lunge attack is anticipated, parry with a step forward to stop the attack unexpectedly early. The riposte is then delivered at close distance.

Direct and Indirect Hits

Direct Hits

Direct hits may be launched as attacks from an engaged blade or covered line, or as ripostes, but all hitting actions should be launched at a moment when the opponent is unready to deal with them. This is why the objectives on page 33 are not only technical, but also prompt the fencer to develop observational and tactical skills.

Direct hits may also be launched from 'absence of blades' and in this case it is absolutely essential to have impeccable timing. Such a direct attack must utilise the precise moment that the opponent is incapable, hesitant or distracted. The execution of a simple direct attack must be exactly that – simple – with no extraneous action of blade, hand or foot, nor any deviation from the line of attack.

These opportune moments usually manifest themselves when the opponent is either (1) preparing an attack, (2) recovering from an attack or riposte, or (3) recovering from an exploration or preparation. (See Fig. 13.) These moments are brief and require instant recognition and prompt delivery of a committed attack. They may be delivered as a reaction but also as an act of 'first intention'. (See Part 4, 'First Intention'.)

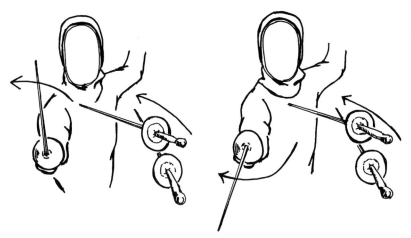

Time the attack at the moment of the opponent's release of the blade.

Fig. 13

Exercises

Fencer B: engage quarte.
Fencer A: remain passive.
Fencer B: change engagement.
Fencer A: remain passive.
Fencer B: release blade.
Fencer A: direct attack with step or lunge.

⋆

Fencer B: step forward from sixte to octave.
Fencer A: step back from sixte to octave.
Fencer B: step forward from octave to sixte.
Fencer A: step back from octave to sixte.
Fencer B: step forward from sixte to octave.
Fencer A: direct attack with step or lunge.

⋆

Fencer A: make a false attack by stepping forward with engagement and direct feint.

Fencer B: parry quarte and step back, releasing Fencer A's blade.

Fencer A: sometimes return to guard but sometimes launch a direct lunge at the moment that the opponent releases the blade.

★

Fencer A: engage sixte.

Fencer B: change engagement and perform direct attack with lunge.

Fencer A: step back with or without parry.

Fencer B: recover.

Fencer A: sometimes attack as the opponent is in mid-recovery.

Indirect Hits

These are executed during an opponent's attempted engagement or change of engagement in order to evade that action and commence an attack.

There are three forms: (1) a disengagement to escape an engagement or to evade a lateral blade action (see Fig. 14a.); (2) counter-disengagement to avoid a circular action (see Fig. 14b); (3) a cut-over to avoid either. (See Fig. 15.)

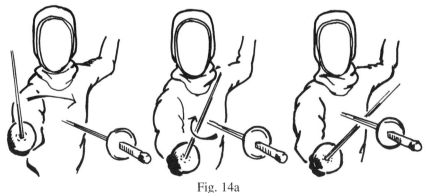

Fig. 14a

A disengagement on the opponent's attempted engagement in quarte.

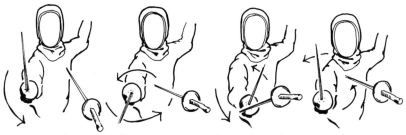

A counter-disengagement on the opponent's attempted
circular engagement in sixte.

Fig. 14b

The disengagement may be completed with a direct, angulated
or opposition thrust.

As with direct attacks the choice of timing is crucial to the success
of indirect attacks. For disengagements and counter-
disengagements to be effective they should be executed as the
opponent is in the process of forming a preparatory blade action,
and at a moment where the opponent has not begun an offensive
action. The extension should be simultaneous with the evasion
so that as the opponent completes his blade action, he finds
himself not only deceived, but also receiving the attack. In order
to achieve this it is necessary for the point movement to be
minimal, passing as close as possible under the opponent's hand,
with no lateral or circular action from the attacker's arm, but
delivered with a smooth rising extension. The manipulation of
the point controlled not by the wrist or forearm but by the fingers
clearly precedes the extension delivered from the tricep.

The cut-over is formed by lifting the point of the blade (the
action is performed from the fingers and with a loose wrist) such
that it passes over the opponent's blade, and, as the point begins
to drop, the extension from the elbow and rising hand delivers
the hit.

Although indirect attacks may be executed from the opponent's
engagement they are best timed on the opponent's change of
engagement, which may be induced by the use of a light grazing
action or pressure (see Part 3, 'Graze Attacks' and 'Pressure').

Fig. 15

Game Practice

With a partner, starting outside lunging distance, play a game where either fencer may advance into fencing distance with a guard or engagement. The two fencers then attempt to seek an advantageous engagement so that they are 'covered' and the opponent is not. After a few mutual changes of engagement, either fencer may break off by retreating out of distance or they may attempt to deceive with an indirect offensive blade action. (If subjected to an attack, a fencer should try to defend by using distance rather than a parry.)

★

Practise as above but the fencers can choose (1) to break off by retreating; (2) to launch a direct thrust from engagement; or (3) to launch a thrust by disengagement or counter-disengagement. Again, if subjected to an attack a fencer should try to step back out of fencing distance.

★

Each fencer should also strive to:

improve blade control and spatial awareness,

find the moments from which an attack can be launched and to realise the time available,

build the ability to move safely into and out of fencing distance,

observe the opponent's habits and level of skill to discover how the opponent responds to threats, that is, the extension, direct or indirect.

Exercises

Fencer A: engage the opponent's blade in quarte.
Fencer B: change the engagement with a circular action.
Fencer A: counter-disengage with extension and step or lunge to hit. The hit may be delivered direct or with an opposition in quarte.

*

Fencer B: step forward with an engagement in sixte.
Fencer A: change the engagement with a circular action.
Fencer B: respond with a pressure.
Fencer A: disengage with extension and lunge (alternatively employ a cut-over).

Against a fencer of the same handedness the correct line of extension in sixte will ensure that a natural line of opposition is formed, otherwise there exists the danger of receiving a hit on the arm or mask should the opponent extend their blade in response to the attack. Against a fencer of the opposite handedness the thrust may be delivered in the line of sixte or in quarte opposition.

*

Fencer B: on guard in octave.

Fencer A: step forward to engage in octave.

Fencer B: change the engagement in the low line (octave if left-handed, septime if right-handed).

Fencer A: disengage extension into the high line with step or lunge.

*

Fencer B: engage quarte with a step forward and change the engagement to sixte (double engagement).

Fencer A: step back as Fencer B initiates the step and then cut-over attack as Fencer B attempts the change of engagement to sixte.

*

Fencer B: from engagement in octave raise blade to sixte.

Fencer A: engage the opponent's blade in quarte and gently graze forward.

Fencer B: change the engagement with a circular action.

Fencer A: counter-disengage with extension and step or lunge to hit with low angulation.

*

Fencer B: step forward with a quarte engagement.

Fencer A: change the engagement with a circular action and gently graze forward.

Fencer B: change the engagement with either a circular action or lateral pressure.

Fencer A: choose the appropriate indirect attack.

*

Fencer B: on guard in octave.

Fencer A: from sixte, step forward to engage septime.

Fencer B: either evade Fencer A's attempted engagement with a disengage attack to high line or permit Fencer A's engagement and then change the engagement with a circular action in the low line.

Fencer A: parry quarte or evade Fencer B's change of engagement as appropriate.

Note that you should never start an indirect attack from the opponent's engagement as they will be in a position of readiness; commence when they are occupied with a movement.

Part 2: Making Progress

Indirect Ripostes

Fig. 16a

Riposte by disengage.

Riposte by cut-over.

Fig. 16b

As with direct ripostes, steady control of the blade and hand at the conclusion of the parry is essential. The weapon should not be held too strongly, nor should the hand and weapon be permitted to move more than is necessary to successfully deflect the attacking blade.

The attacker's response to the failure of the attack and subsequent exposure to a direct riposte will motivate them to protect their target by withdrawing the arm and blade to form a parry. The successful defender can observe the line of defence taken by the attacker by resting in their parry and can choose an indirect riposte, either passing under the opponent's blade with a disengage or counter-disengage (see Fig. 16a), or over the blade with a cut-over (see Fig. 16b).

Exercise

Fencer A: engage quarte.
Fencer B: change engagement with a circular action, extend and lunge.
Fencer A: parry with circular quarte and pause in the parry.
Fencer B: take a (premature) parry of sixte or quarte.
Fencer A: riposte indirect with disengage or cut-over and step back.

Fencing Distance

Following a successful parry, one danger that exists for the overeager fencer is the instinct to close distance with the opponent to deliver a riposte. This often occurs when the riposte is indirect or compound and the fencer has released the opponent's blade from the parry but not finally determined the nature of the riposte or the target. In so advancing in this opportunistic manner the defender delays the final action of the riposte and is put at risk. This unnecessary advance is usually triggered by the sight of the original attacker commencing the recovery and the thought that he or she might escape. However, it should be borne in mind that an attack delivered from lunging distance will recover to that same distance, that is, the original attacker is always in range and can be hit with a lunge as the recovery is completed. A step forward is, therefore, totally unnecessary and would bring the fencers too close.

The correct response is to rely on the speed of the riposting blade and hand to hit the target before it is out of arm's reach. If this is not achieved then the recovering opponent can be pursued with an additional blade action delivered with a lunge or flèche (see Part 2, 'Compound Ripostes' and Part 4, 'The Redouble'), or the opponent can be attacked just at the moment when they are concluding their recovery.

Having said that it is inappropriate to advance in order to *commence* a riposte, there is nothing amiss with using a step or half-step to *conclude* the riposte on a fencer who is unable to complete the recovery to full distance. Nor would it be inappropriate to advance in the parry with the security of holding the opposing blade in order to deliver a controlled riposte at close quarters (see Part 5: Additional Combat Skills).

Blade Manipulation: Transports

The four hand and blade positions considered so far (sixte, quarte, octave and septime) are referred to as 'supinated', with the knuckles resting vertically or partly turned under the handle. For each supinated hand position there is a corresponding 'pronated' hand position where the knuckles are uppermost. Those shown in Figure 17 are 'tierce', 'seconde' and 'prime'.

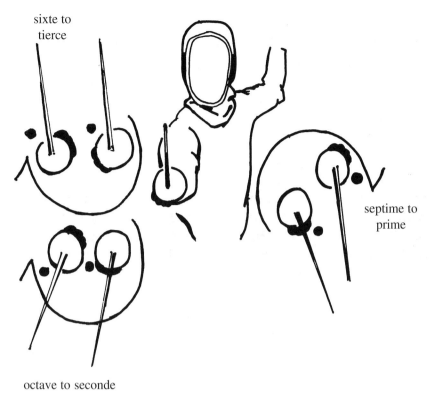

sixte to
tierce

septime to
prime

octave to seconde

The pronated guards.

Fig. 17

They are achieved by rotating the hand and are usually performed with a small, simultaneous movement away from the body. In the case of prime the final height of the position may vary. A rotation of quarte, bringing the knuckles uppermost, is also possible but is not illustrated. This position is known as 'quinte' at foil.

Pronated hand positions are mainly used in actions at close quarters and to form angulated hits. However, they need to be introduced at this stage because of the association of seconde and prime with a further supinated position, that of 'high' or 'high sixte', which is discussed below.

In order to locate and practise the first three pronated blade positions, place a partner's blade against the outside forte and shell of the foil and rotate the hand as shown above. The rotation will bring the thumb to a position where it directly opposes the opponent's blade and so gives greater firmness to the position.

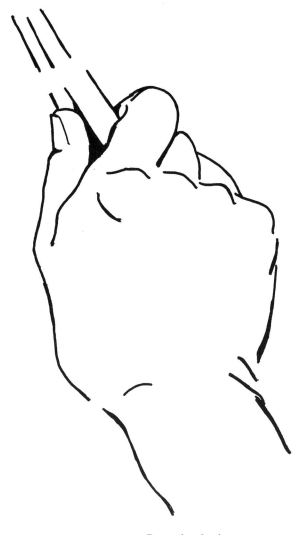

Pronation in tierce.

Fig. 18

Exercise

Fencer B: engage sixte and on Fencer A's pressure, attack by disengage.

Fencer A: parry with circular sixte and as Fencer B rests in the lunge, pronate the hand to tierce, pushing outwards slightly, step forward and hit with pronated angulation.

Figure 19 shows the high sixte guard or parry, which is an additional supinated position that gives protection against hits and threats descending to the target, as in the case of cut-overs. The hand position is similar to septime but the hand is raised on the sixte side of the body. From this high guard or parry it is often more effective to take seconde when a subsequent parry is needed, and from seconde, prime is the natural lateral parry.

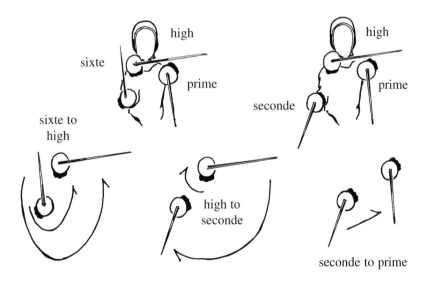

Fig. 19

Practise forming the following guards or parries against a partner's disengage, angulated, cut-over, or flick-like hits at your target: sixte to high sixte, high sixte to seconde, seconde to prime.

As sixte and octave are the usual guards for a lesson or the commencement of a bout, the other guards tend to be less well exploited as initial positions. A fencer who has been subjected to attacks may well prefer to adopt a guard that covers the target that has been the final focus of an attack and so frustrate further similar attacks. For example, a guard of high sixte against a fencer who has habitually attacked with cut-overs. Alternatively, quarte or septime against a fencer who continually attacks those lines. By adopting the appropriate guard the initiative is taken from the opponent whose only choice is then to seek attacks to less favoured targets. For today's fencer the ability to commence offensive actions or defensive strategies from the high sixte guard is becoming as necessary as the traditional importance placed on the mastery of sixte.

Additional to the high sixte parry or guard is the position of 'high septime'. (See Fig. 20.) This is achieved simply by rotating the hand fractionally more and elevating from the position of septime. Its most frequent use is to lift an opposing blade from septime either because the parry is somewhat insecure, or to create a greater target for the riposte.

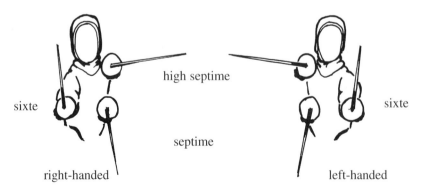

Fig. 20

Exercises

Fencer A: step and engage quarte, then change to sixte (double engagement).
Fencer B: cut-over lunge.
Fencer A: parry high, riposte direct or indirect, and step back.

★

Fencer A: engage sixte.
Fencer B: cut-over attack by step.
Fencer A: step back and parry high sixte, then pause.
Fencer B: from extension, disengage lunge to flank.
Fencer A: parry seconde (stepping back) and riposte to the opponent's back.

★

Fencer A: from Fencer B's engagement, change of engagement to quarte.
Fencer B: counter disengage extension and lunge.
Fencer A: as the opponent's point passes under the hand, take a septime parry, and *either* riposte immediately *or* lift the blade to high septime and riposte, *or* pause momentarily before pronating the hand to prime whilst retaining blade contact. Then step forward inside the opponent's reach, release contact with the blade and deliver an angulated hit.

★

Fencer A: circular change of engagement.
Fencer B: disengage extension under Fencer A's forearm and lunge at flank.
Fencer A: parry octave and *either* riposte immediately by lifting the point in a semicircle and hitting the chest or the exposed shoulder or back, *or* pronate the hand to seconde whilst retaining blade contact, then step forward inside the opponent's reach and deliver an angulated hit.

★

Fencer B: step forward lunge with low extension angulating the point upwards.

Fencer A: from sixte step back, lowering the point and take a high septime parry (Figs. 21a and 21b) and riposte. The action is one of gathering the opponent's point from beneath.

Note that a parry finishing in high sixte as opposed to high septime is not appropriate in this instance as only a high septime will give the necessary opposition of forte to foible to ensure a secure parry.

★

High septime against a low-angled attack (side view).

Fig. 21a

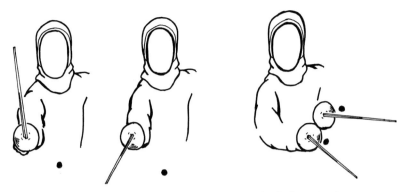

High septime against a low-angled attack (facing view).

Fig. 21b

Against a fencer of the opposite handedness:

Fencer A: engage quarte.
Fencer B: disengage extension and lunge.
Fencer A: parry circular quarte and riposte immediately with an arc-like point movement (similar to a cut-over) to deliver an angulated flick either to the shoulder, back or flank (see the cover illustration). Alternatively, pause momentarily in the quarte parry, then, maintaining blade contact, step forward inside the opponent's reach, release contact with their blade by inverting yours from quarte to prime (pivoting on a point some twenty centimetres above the opponent's blade) and use the momentum of the inversion to deliver an angulated flick to the chest.

Note that this inversion is the same as that shown in Figure 43 on page 119, the difference being that in this instance the fencer making the riposte is advancing, whereas in the later illustration it is the attacker who is advancing. The concept of inverting from quarte to prime remains the same.

*

Fencer A: engage sixte.
Fencer B: disengage and lunge.

Fencer A: parry septime then pronate to prime and step forward.

Fencer B: recover blade to sixte to maintain opposition of the blades.

Fencer A: from prime deliver a cut-over (inverted) to the chest.

Second Intention: The First Counter-Riposte

'Second intention' is when a fencer attacks without the intention of scoring with the attack because they have predicted the opponent's defence and thought one move ahead. The attack is simply to draw the opponent's defence and subsequent known response, which is then exploited with a second offensive action.

It contrasts to 'first intention' where the offensive is launched without regard to any later reaction or tactical action, and where full confidence and commitment is given to the initial offensive. The first counter-riposte can be used as an act of second intention.

In Figure 22, after perceiving that the opponent tends to respond automatically with a parry of quarte and direct riposte, the fencer lunges with the sword arm fully extended but loose and relaxed. The defender forms a parry and commences the riposte but, being anticipated, it falls into the quarte parry taken on the lunge by the original attacker.

The attacker then ripostes in turn (counter-riposte) at the now exposed target of the defender.

The riposte shown is direct but it could equally well be delivered as a disengage, a cut-over or compound. To be effective, the original attack, although false, has to be delivered at a realistic distance and with realistic timing if it is to draw the desired response. The parry of quarte on the lunge is performed with a deeper flex of elbow and wrist, and a higher hand in relation to the body than when performed on guard.

Fig. 22

First counter-riposte.

Fig. 22 cont.

Exercises

Fencer A: engage quarte.
Fencer B: circular change of engagement.
Fencer A: counter-disengage with extension and lunge.
Fencer B: lateral parry followed by direct riposte.
Fencer A: from lunge, parry quarte, counter-riposte direct
and recover.

★

Fencer A: engage octave then detach from the blade to lunge in the high line.

Fencer B: parry sixte (parry quarte if of the opposite handedness to Fencer A) and riposte to shoulder.

Fencer A: from lunge, parry high sixte, counter-riposte and recover.

*

Fencer A: engage sixte and direct lunge.

Fencer B: step back with circular parry and riposte by disengage.

Fencer A: in the lunge either form a lateral parry of sixte or take a parry of high sixte and riposte direct. Alternatively, from the parry of sixte the counter-riposte may be made by disengage or cut-over.

*

Fencer A: make a light quarte engagement then, with detachment, extend direct and step forward as a false attack.

Fencer B: respond with an immediate lateral parry and direct riposte (moving out of distance).

Fencer A: parry quarte and counter-riposte direct with step. Alternatively, Fencer A may parry with high sixte (instead of quarte) and counter-riposte, or Fencer B may step back from the riposte, in which case Fencer A completes the counter-riposte with a lunge.

When employing a first counter-riposte against an opponent of the opposite handedness who parries in quarte, the defender has a distinct advantage as the original attacker is held on their back hand. Consequently the most direct response, a parry of sixte, is comparatively weak, whilst a circular parry of quarte could take too long. More effective would be to use high sixte or to rotate the hand to prime in order to introduce the counter-riposte.

Exercise

Fencer A: beat disengage half-lunge as a false attack.
Fencer B: quarte riposte direct.
Fencer A: parry high septime, recover forward and riposte
or parry prime, close distance and riposte.

Compound Offensive Actions

A compound attack or riposte is one delivered with one or more
feints in order to deceive a parry or parries. Mastery of the
technique and timing of simple direct and indirect offensive
actions is a necessary prerequisite to the successful
accomplishment of compound attacks and ripostes.

Compound Attacks

In Figure 23 the attacker engages sixte and gives a slight pressure,
then disengages from the opponent's return pressure,
simultaneously extending towards the lower target.

Perceiving an attack in the low line, the defender responds with
a parry of octave. However, the attacker has premeditated this
response and deceives by disengaging back to the high line with
a lunge in order to hit the target in the high line.

Please note that in order to illustrate clearly the concept of a
compound attack, the degree of movement of the attacker's arm
has been exaggerated. In reality the hand should move
continuously towards the target with only the blade misdirecting
the opponent.

A compound attack may be initiated with either a direct,
disengage, counter-disengage, or cut-over feint. Whichever feint
is chosen, it should be launched at a moment when the opponent
is preoccupied and unready to deal with it. The opponent's
resultant parry should be deceived, passing the point around the

foil guard with minimal blade action. During the feint the point penetrates at least as far as the opponent's fingers so that the distance to be covered and the time taken for the final delivery of the hit is within the reaction time of the opponent.

A compound attack.

Fig. 23

The key to a successful compound attack lies not only in the timing of the feint but also in the timing and finesse of the final deception. This latter timing will depend on the level and ability of the opponent. A less experienced opponent will tend to parry immediately, whilst a more experienced opponent will delay the parry. The result is that the fencer should strive to practise compound attacks with the feints penetrating to various depths. In practice bouts, false attacks can be used to determine not only the nature of the opponent's parry but also the timing.

In the exercises that follow, once the mechanics of the blade have been mastered, practise with variations in the timing of the parry. For example, the defender can parry immediately on the feint, or, in another practice, the defender only parries if the feint is accompanied with a lunge.

The tidy control of the blade at the moment of deception is crucial, for, having closed the distance between the point and the target, and having gained an advantage in timing over the opponent, it can all be wasted if the deception is greater in time and distance than that needed by the defender to form another parry.

The maintenance of balance when using a lunge is very important. If your body weight moves over the leading leg during the feint, then gravity will prematurely foreshorten the lunge. When practising, the feint can be accompanied with a half-step, the heel just lightly touching the ground, and then the deception can be accompanied by accelerating the completion of the lunge.

When advancing with a preparation and then attacking, there are several combinations of foot and blade actions, and the following exercises should be adapted to include a range of footwork:

- engagement on the front foot followed by feint on the rear foot, deception and lunge (against an early response and for basic skills learning).

- engagement on the front foot, complete the step, feint, deception and lunge, (against a later response).
- engagement on the front foot, complete the step, feint with a step, deception and lunge (against a late response as the partner moves away).

The most common form of compound attack is the one-two, which is formed of two disengagements to deceive the opponent's lateral actions. The other classic compound attack is the doublé, which is formed of two counter-disengagements to deceive the opponent's circular actions.

If an opponent tends to overreact defensively or is caught off-guard, it is possible to successfully employ feints with a bent arm provided that the point is progressing forward and distance is being gained continuously. However, a fault of many novices in early bouts is the failure to extend and penetrate with the feint. They then adopt a series of bent-arm disengagements followed by a lunge; in reality this is a preparation followed by a simple attack with no distance or timing having been gained.

Exercises

Fencer A: step forward with an engagement in quarte or sixte.
Fencer B: circular change of engagement.
Fencer A: counter-disengage with extension (feint).
Fencer B: circular parry.
Fencer A: deceive with a counter-disengagement and lunge (doublé).

⋆

Fencer B: step forward with an engagement in quarte or sixte.
Fencer A: circular change of engagement.

Fencer B: lateral pressure to change engagement.
Fencer A: disengage with extension (feint).
Fencer B: lateral parry.
Fencer A: deceive with a disengagement and lunge (one-two).

*

Fencer A: step forward with a double-engagement (quarte then sixte).
Fencer B: respond with a pressure.
Fencer A: disengage with extension.
Fencer B: lateral parry.
Fencer A: deceive with a disengagement and lunge.

*

Fencer A: in septime or octave.
Fencer B: step forward to engage octave.
Fencer A: deceive the engagement and feint to the opponent's chest.
Fencer B: parry sixte or quarte.
Fencer A: choose the appropriate disengage and lunge.

*

Fencer A: step forward with an engagement in sixte.
Fencer B: step back, evading the engagement and maintaining a sixte guard.
Fencer A: step forward with a feint direct.
Fencer B: perform two successive lateral parries.
Fencer A: deceive with a one-two and lunge.
(Fencers A and B have the same handedness.)

*

Fencer A: step forward with sixte and, on Fencer B's pressure, feint of disengagement.
Fencer B: perform two successive lateral parries.
Fencer A: deceive with a one-two and lunge.

*

Fencer A: from engagement of quarte, extend to feint direct, drop point below height of opponent's hand, smoothly commence the lunge with the front leg extension as if attacking the opponent's flank.

Fencer B: when Fencer A has commenced their lunge, parry octave.

Fencer A: deceive the parry of octave with a disengagement to the high line, simultaneously thrusting from the rear leg to accelerate the conclusion of the attack (progressive compound attack).

Multiple feints and deceptions, although not pertinent to the bout, are useful training aids for the development of point control, timing, balance and mobility. These practices include 'doublé-de-doublé', which is two successive doublés in opposite directions, and 'doublé-one-two', which is self-explanatory.

Compound Ripostes

Look again at the indirect ripostes in Figures 16a and 16b. The successful defender, relaxing their blade but maintaining the parry position, observes the defensive blade direction taken by the opponent and then deceives it with an indirect riposte. However, it could be that the opponent has fast reactions and good blade control and, therefore, the ability to parry the indirect riposte. This second parry will normally be a lateral parry because of the lack of time in which to do anything else.

Such successive parries can be deceived by employing two or more indirect actions, although two should be sufficient.

Figure 24 shows a riposte from quarte with two disengagements ('riposte by one-two') to deceive the opponent's instinctive lateral parries. Note that the hand remains on the quarte side of the body during the first disengagement, which becomes a feint, and, unlike a compound attack, there is no extension because of the proximity of the opponent. Once the second disengagement has commenced, the sword hand travels towards the sixte side and rises to extend and deliver the hit.

Fig. 24

This assumes that the attacker has remained on the lunge. In the event that the attacker recovers from the lunge as they form the first parry, then the first action of the riposte (the feint of disengagement) will need to be performed with an extension, and the final action will need to be delivered with a lunge. In other words, the compound riposte takes on the qualities of a compound attack.

As with indirect ripostes, the successful defender should not resist the opponent's blade but, resting in the parry, feel the detachment or light pressure which will give an early tactile indication of the opponent's intended parry.

An immediate direct feint should not be given as this is obviously in the same line and with the same timing as a direct riposte and would therefore be parried. However, a riposte with feint direct that is delayed until the opponent is in the final completion of the recovery can be successful; the timing is more that of an attack on the opponent's recovery. Another variation is to employ a riposte by broken time. (See Part 3, 'Broken Time'.)

Exercises

Fencer A: engage quarte.
Fencer B: circular change of engagement, extend and lunge.
Fencer A: circular parry of quarte and riposte direct.
Fencer B: lateral parry on the lunge and direct riposte.
Fencer A: lateral parry.
Fencer B: two lateral parries on the lunge.
Fencer A: riposte by one-two and step back.

*

Fencer B: step engage in quarte.
Fencer A: step back.
Fencer B: step forward maintaining quarte engagement.
Fencer A: circular change of engagement.
Fencer B: counter-disengagement with extension and lunge.
Fencer A: circular parry.
Fencer B: on the lunge take two lateral parries.
Fencer A: riposte with two cut-overs (double cut-over).

*

Fencer B: from quarte engagement release opponent's blade.
Fencer A: direct lunge.
Fencer B: parry quarte and riposte direct.
Fencer A: on the lunge second intention quarte parry followed by counter-riposte with one-two.

*

Fencer A: from quarte engagement release opponent's blade.
Fencer B: direct lunge and recover with a circular parry.
Fencer A: parry quarte and feint with counter-disengage and extension.
Fencer B: circular parry.
Fencer A: complete the compound riposte with a counter-disengage and lunge.

*

Fencer A: from quarte engagement release opponent's blade.
Fencer B: direct lunge and recover either to quarte or sixte followed by a circular parry.
Fencer A: parry quarte and feint with either disengage or counter-disengage extension as appropriate, then complete the compound riposte, lunging with counter-disengage.

*

Fencer A: from sixte engagement release opponent's blade.
Fencer B: direct lunge and recover to sixte (followed by lateral parries).
Fencer A: parry high septime; at the moment Fencer B completes the recovery to sixte, feint direct and, lunging, deceive the lateral parries with a one-two.

Consolidation Exercises

Fencer B: engage sixte.
Fencer A: change engagement with lateral pressure.
Fencer B: *either* take a circular change of engagement followed by a circular parry *or* take a lateral change of engagement followed by a circular parry.
Fencer A: *either* doublé lunge *or* attack with disengage, counter-disengage.

*

Fencer A: step forward with double engagement quarte-sixte.
Fencer B: *either* give pressure followed by a lateral parry *or* disengage attack on Fencer A's attempted quarte engagement.
Fencer A: compound attack with one-two or parry and riposte.

*

Fencer A: advance with double engagement quarte-sixte, followed by cut-over lunge.

Fencer B: *either* parry quarte and riposte direct *or* parry high septime and riposte disengaging low.

Fencer A: parry quarte and counter-riposte.

★

Fencer B: engage sixte and direct lunge.

Fencer A: parry quarte and riposte by cut-over.

Fencer B: *either* lateral parry and riposte by disengage *or* high sixte parry and riposte.

Fencer A: *either* lateral parry and riposte by disengage or by one-two *or* parry with seconde and riposte as appropriate.

★

Fencer B: in octave.

Fencer A: step with octave engagement.

Fencer B: *either* disengage to the high line with a lunge *or* step back in sixte and respond to Fencer A's engagement with a change of engagement *or* step back in sixte and respond to Fencer A's engagement with a change of engagement together with another step back.

Fencer A: *either* parry (sixte, quarte or high septime) and riposte *or* step with engagement of quarte and launch an indirect or compound attack with lunge *or* step with engagement of quarte and launch a compound attack with a step and lunge.

Part 3: More Blade and Footwork

Half-Steps

When manoeuvring it is necessary to have the ability to stop and/or change direction suddenly. This can be accomplished by the use of half-steps. Normally, in order to complete the step, the rear foot immediately follows the front when moving forward, and the front foot follows the rear when retiring. In a half-step only the leading foot action is performed and the second part of the step remains incomplete. The objective is to disrupt the opponent's sense of distance and timing.

Examples

Step back and then follow this with a half-step back using only the rear foot. Immediately return to guard. If the opponent is following your retirement they will suddenly find themselves too close and without the initiative.

Step forward and then follow this with a half-step forward using only the front foot. Immediately return to guard. If the opponent retires they will find that they are out of distance.

Proceed as above two or three times so that the opponent becomes unsure and hesitates to move out of distance. Then, from the half-step, advance rapidly and accelerate the rear foot action of the step to launch an attack.

Engage sixte with a half-step forward. The opponent employs a circular change of engagement with a step forward. Counter-disengage and lunge immediately from the half-step position. With the closing distance there is neither the time nor the space to complete a full step and deliver the attack successfully.

The Flèche

An offensive action can not only be delivered with a step or lunge but also with a flèche. (See Fig. 25.) This action requires total commitment and excellent timing. The front foot remains in place as the blade and sword arm are extended towards the opponent. The extension draws the body forward and a vigorous extension of the front leg launches the attack.

The flèche.

Fig. 25

The fencer should endeavour to extend in a line from the sword hand, through the armpit, ribcage and along the upper thigh to the toe. At the very moment of reaching this maximum extension, which will occupy only a fraction of a second, the hit should arrive on the opponent. This will be at the moment when the feet are about to pass; the rear foot then continues in advance of the attacker to enable a safe landing. By the time the rear foot lands, the hit will have been delivered and the sword arm will be retracting to a quarte parry as the fencer regains equilibrium.

The flèche may be very effectively delivered from a half-step forward. (See Fig. 26.) An engagement or feint may accompany the half-step, which is followed by the smooth acceleration of the delivery of the attack. The absence of both footwork and the usual rhythm of a step-lunge attack has the effect of slowing the defender's reaction.

The flèche preceded by a half-step.

Fig. 26

The flèche may also be preceded by a withdrawal of the front foot just ahead of the arm extension in order to attack into the opponent's closing distance. (See Fig. 27.)

Fig. 27

Exercises

Fencer A: step with an engagement in quarte.
Fencer B: circular change of engagement.
Fencer A: counter-disengagement with flèche.

★

Fencer A: step with an engagement in octave.
Fencer B: give pressure.
Fencer A: disengage to the high line and flèche.

★

Fencer B: engage quarte and change to sixte.
Fencer A: remain passive.
Fencer B: release blade.
Fencer A: direct attack with flèche.

★

Fencer A: engage sixte.
Fencer B: change engagement and perform direct attack with lunge.
Fencer A: step back with or without parry.
Fencer B: recover.
Fencer A: flèche as the opponent is in mid-recovery.

★

Fencer B: double engagement quarte-sixte with a step forward.
Fencer A: step back as Fencer B initiates the step and then cut-over flèche on the attempted change of engagement to sixte.

Actions on the Blade

In order to prepare the way for an attack the blade actions so far described are those of 'engagement'. The other actions available include 'beats', 'grazes', and 'broken time'. Beats and grazes make contact with the opponent's blade and require the spatial skills inherent in engagements, whilst broken time avoids the opponent's blade and requires some of the timing skills inherent in compound offensive actions.

Beat Attacks

A beat attack is a short, sharp beating action on the opponent's blade in one of the fencing guards or lines. The direction and position are similar to an engagement but with only momentary contact as the attacker's blade rebounds from the struck blade to deliver an immediate attack or feint.

From a sixte guard the blade can be directed in a circle to sixte or a semicircle to octave, with the hand moving slightly forward and slightly to the outside. Alternatively the blade can be directed to quarte, septime or high, again with a forward action of the hand and accompanied by a partial rotation, although the hand should not travel across the body as if fully forming a guard.

The attacker should direct his or her blade at the point in space where it is anticipated that contact will be made, and the action should recoil from that point with the hand accelerating and rising as the extension is completed. In other words, a correctly formed beat action relies on momentum (kinetic energy) and the rapid transfer of that energy to dislodge the opposing blade. It does not rely on force of leverage to carry the opposing blade out of position.

Endeavouring to strike the opponent's blade with the edge rather than the flat of one's own blade will help to achieve a suitable degree of rotation and to maximise the impact of the beat.

From a quarte guard a circular quarte beat can be effective, as can a semicircular septime beat. The hand can rest in quarte or advance slightly for the execution of the former, but needs to advance for the septime beat. A beat with pronation to seconde is more effective than an octave beat from quarte. Additionally, the seconde beat is very effective when launched from an engagement of high sixte against the opponent's automatic disengagement.

The purpose of the beat is either to dislodge the opponent's blade, making way for a direct attack, or to stimulate a response that can be exploited with an indirect or compound attack, or an act of second intention.

Exercises

Fencer A: engage sixte.
Fencer B: disengage to absence of blades.
Fencer A: quarte beat lunge.

*

Fencer B: step forward in quarte followed by a circular parry.
Fencer A: change beat, counter-disengage attack by lunge or flèche.

*

Fencer A: step forward with double engagement sixte-quarte.
Fencer B: detach blade to octave.
Fencer A: septime beat lunge.

*

Fencer B: step forward with extension from sixte.
Fencer A: from sixte beat high septime and feint or attack.

*

Fencer A: step forward with quarte beat extension as a feint. (Note the beat extension takes place as the front foot commences the step.)

Fencer B: parry the feint with quarte and riposte direct in place.

Fencer A: parry either with quarte or high sixte and riposte with step or short lunge.

Beats and Steps

When preparing attacks with beats whilst advancing, the correct coordination of hand and foot is essential. For a direct attack with a step and lunge, the blade should not commit to the beat during the advance of the front foot, the beat should be timed a fraction of a second ahead of the rear foot landing on the floor. An earlier beat would give the defender more time in which to form a parry. If a jump forward (balestra) is used to launch an attack, then, likewise, the beat is a fraction ahead of the landing of the feet.

When a beat is used to prepare a compound attack, then the beat is simultaneous with the front foot movement. This gives time for both the feint and deception at the completion of the step and development of the lunge.

Exercise

Fencer A: beat extend, advancing the front foot.

Fencer B: step back with a circular parry, then take a lateral parry.

Fencer A: counter-disengage in completing the step, followed by a disengage lunge or flèche.

★

Fencer A: step forward with engagement of high (hand slightly advanced and timed with the advance of the front foot).

Fencer B: on Fencer A's attempted engagement, evade with disengagement.

Fencer A: in completing the step, seconde beat and lunge to upper target.

Through or Grazing Beats

This form of beat does not have the quality of a rebound as before but the action is that of a slicing or grazing movement against and up the opponent's blade (a little like a cymbal being struck). The action is, in effect, a combination of the beat and a cut-over. As with other preparations, its purpose is to paralyse or misdirect the opponent in order to launch a direct, indirect or compound attack.

Useful among these actions are:

- from sixte, against an opponent on guard in a high line, a beating action towards quarte, slicing over the opponent's blade with the attack or feint delivered with angulation from a pronated hand position (quinte).

- from sixte, a circular beating action, again slicing over the opponent's blade and this time with the attack or feint delivered towards the top (or even the rear) of the opponent's shoulder.

- from sixte or quarte, against an opponent on guard in a low line, a beating action through the line of septime to finish with a feint or attack in the high line. (See Fig. 28.)

Through beat of septime (two views).

Fig. 28

This latter action against a fencer advancing with multiple feints in the low line can be used as a parry whereas a conventional opposition parry could easily be deceived.

Graze Attacks

These are more subtle actions on the opponent's blade. From a light engagement, rather than give an obvious pressure or beat on the opposing blade, the point gently slides down towards the opponent's forte with a slight and gentle advance of the sword hand. This induces a sense of uncertainty or insecurity in the opponent so that they will begin to cover with a lateral or circular change of engagement. At this point the attacker launches a lunge or flèche with the appropriate evasion. It is also entirely possible that the opponent hesitates, unsure of the sensation of the graze, thus giving an opportunity for a direct flèche attack.

The advantage of this grazing action is that it permits the hand to make early progress towards the target and helps to maintain small controlled deceptions. It is therefore a useful training tool to build the fencer's hand technique and coordination.

Exercises

Fencer B: step forward in octave.
Fencer A: through beat septime to the high line, step forward to hit.

★

Fencer B: advance with multiple feints in the low line.
Fencer A: step back in sixte and take a through beat of septime and hits to the upper target whilst continuously retiring.

★

Fencer A: step forward with a through beat in quarte (the hand will finish in quinte).

Fencer B: *either* remain passive *or* threaten with an extension (stop-hit) *or* parry octave.

Fencer A: complete the attack to the low target under Fencer B's sword arm *or* parry with high sixte, sixte and riposte, *or* deceive the octave parry with a disengage over Fencer B's sword arm to the upper target.

★

Against a fencer of the opposite handedness:

Fencer A: step forward with a through beat in quarte (that is, against the opponent's sixte position).

Fencer B: parry quarte.

Fencer A: cut-over attack.

Alternatively, Fencer A can pause following the quarte through beat, delaying the attack, and, if Fencer B parries quarte and then returns to guard in sixte, the attack can be delivered as Fencer B returns to sixte (broken time).

★

Fencer B: engage quarte with a step forward.

Fencer A: circular change of engagement followed by a light graze towards Fencer B's forte.

Fencer B: cover in sixte.

Fencer A: disengage flèche.

★

Fencer B: engage sixte with a step forward.

Fencer A: circular change of engagement followed by a light graze towards Fencer B's forte.

Fencer B: lateral or circular change of engagement.

Fencer A: disengage or counter-disengage as appropriate and lunge.

★

Fencer B: engage sixte with a half-step forward.

Fencer A: circular change of engagement followed by a light graze towards Fencer B's forte.

Fencer B: lateral or circular change of engagement with a recovery, followed by a lateral parry.

Fencer A: disengage feint or counter-disengage feint accompanied with a half-step followed by disengage flèche to complete a compound attack.

Pressure

As with graze attacks, it is not necessary to complete a covered engagement as it is sufficient to make light contact preparatory to the attack. Attacks with pressure are successful when the opponent does not respond automatically to an engagement (sensing that they could provoke an indirect or compound attack), but hesitates, usually whilst giving ground. At the moment the attacker senses both the hesitation and sufficient closing of distance, he or she should apply the pressure and extension as one fluid blade action. The hand-foot coordination is similar to that used for a beat; that is, the blade action is during the rear foot movement for a direct attack and earlier for a more complex attack.

The pressure is applied with a slight rotation of the sword hand as the hand commences its advance. The strongest is that applied to a quarte engagement or contact and the action is somewhat like turning a doorknob.

Exercises

Fencer A: advances.

Fencer B: retires.

Fencer A: makes a light engagement in quarte and continues to advance.

Fencer B: continues to retire.

Fencer A: gives pressure in quarte and flèches.

*

Fencer B: retires with the blade in low line.

Fencer A: advances with a light engagement in septime, changes to octave.

Fencer B: continues to retire.

Fencer A: gives pressure in octave and lunges or flèches.

Broken Time

'Broken time' or 'temps perdu' (lost time) is the name given to describe offensive actions where the blade hesitates or pauses in its delivery. These actions exploit the defensive response of the opponent. At the conclusion of a feint, the attacking fencer does not attempt to evade the parry with a disengage, but, in order to avoid contact, removes the blade out of the line of the parry, usually laterally or by drawing back. The response of the defender, coming under attack and not feeling a successful parry, is usually to take a further instinctive parry. At the moment that the defender executes that instinctive parry, the target is exposed. The attacker's blade and point are brought back into line to place the hit.

Broken-time actions may be used as substitutes for compound actions of attack, riposte or renewal. Their effectiveness is not simply in deceiving the opponent with a disengagement or similar, but in evading the blade and simultaneously changing the rhythm or tempo of the attack.

Broken Time as Attack

In Figure 29 Fencer A commences a direct attack by lunge, provoking a lateral parry of quarte from the defender, Fencer B. Fencer A completes the lunge but, instead of disengaging to hit with the completion of the lunge, retracts the arm whilst removing the blade, point lifted, to sixte. Thus the attacker comes to rest in the lunge with a bent arm and blade ready to strike at the moment Fencer B forms an instinctive sixte parry.

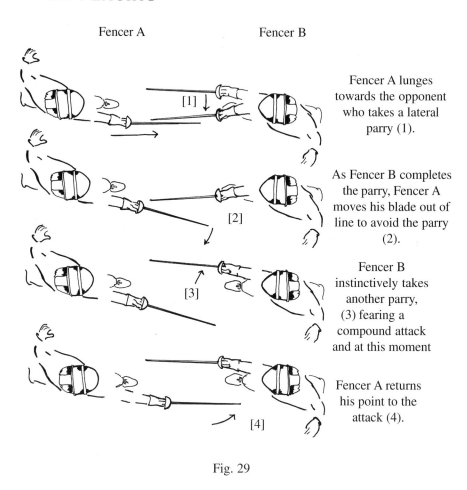

Fencer A   Fencer B

[1]

Fencer A lunges towards the opponent who takes a lateral parry (1).

[2]

As Fencer B completes the parry, Fencer A moves his blade out of line to avoid the parry (2).

[3]

Fencer B instinctively takes another parry, (3) fearing a compound attack and at this moment

[4]

Fencer A returns his point to the attack (4).

Fig. 29

To practise the action and its timing, a fencer can lunge to hit a target and at the moment of hitting immediately retract the point, experimenting with a number of different positions, and, having rested in the lunge, replacing the point on the target. Later the action is repeated, withdrawing the blade at the last possible moment before the initial impact, before practising against a partner who takes successive lateral parries.

Broken-time attacks may be introduced with beats or other actions on the blade. They may also be used to introduce counter-time actions. However, tactically it is advisable to precede them with real or false attacks to discover the reaction and timing of the opponent's defence.

Exercise

Progression 1
Fencer A: attack with lateral quarte beat, lunging with a compound attack of one-two.
Fencer B: employ lateral parries to defeat the attack.

Progression 2
Fencer A: attack with beat disengage lunge and take the point out of line (following the direction of the disengagement) to complete the lunge with a flexed arm.
Fencer B: employ lateral parries as previously.
Fencer A: hit to an exposed target as the defender hesitates.

Against a fencer of the same handedness the hit in Progression 2 could be a hit to the flank below the defender's forearm, the shoulder above the forearm, or with a disengagement to the lower body. Against a fencer of the opposite handedness the hit could be delivered to the lower body, by disengagement to the flank, or by cut-over to the shoulder.

Broken Time as Riposte

There are two moments when the concept of broken time can be successfully employed with the riposte. In the first, the deliberate loss of time occurs immediately following the successful parry. The defender detaches his parry from the blade, but instead of riposting immediately, delays with the point out of line (either moved somewhat laterally, raised or lowered). The opponent's response to form an instinctive parry or parries will expose them to a well-timed delayed riposte.

Alternatively, the riposte may commence with a conventional feint of disengagement or cut-over, but it is at the conclusion of this latter action that the timing is broken in order to exploit the opponent's defensive action.

When employing broken time, both in the attack and riposte, it is essential to acquire the timing of the opponent's defence in order to defeat it. There is the danger that the broken-time action hesitates overlong and allows the opponent to regain the initiative of offence. A less experienced fencer will use broken time to explore rather than exploit the opponent's defence and in doing so will become vulnerable.

Exercises

Fencer A: step with through beat in sixte as feint.

Fencer B: lateral parry and detach with a step back.

Fencer A: step with cut-over-like blade action and direct lunge, breaking time at the end of the lunge to avoid contact with Fencer B's parry.

Fencer B: take two lateral parries or parry high septime and then seconde.

Fencer A: on the lunge, return the point to hit at the moment of Fencer B's exposure.

*

Fencer A: step with lateral engagement.

Fencer B: circular change of engagement followed by a lateral parry.

Fencer A: counter-disengage feint, disengage lunge, then retract the arm and point before the completion of the lunge.

Fencer B: take a second lateral parry.

Fencer A: on the lunge, return the point to hit at the moment of Fencer B's exposure.

*

Fencer A: step forward with a beat and detachment.

Fencer B: step back.

Fencer A: step forward with a through beat in sixte, extending and then immediately retracting the cut-over feint with a half-step (that is, only the front foot is advanced in the step).

Fencer B: parry high septime and then seconde.

Fencer A: as Fencer B takes seconde, complete the lunge direct.

★

Fencer B: from Fencer A's engagement, disengage feint and deceive the circular parry.

Fencer A: circular parry followed by lateral parry with detachment lifting the point.

Fencer B: recover to guard with successive lateral parries.

Fencer A: complete broken time cut-over riposte with lunge or flèche.

Consolidation Exercises

Fencer B: change engagement.

Fencer A: remain passive.

Fencer B: release blade.

Fencer A: direct attack with flèche.

★

Fencer A: engage sixte.

Fencer B: change engagement and perform direct attack with lunge.

Fencer A: step back with or without parry.

Fencer B: recover.

Fencer A: sometimes attack by flèche with direct feint and disengage as the opponent is in mid-recovery.

★

Fencer B: on guard in octave.

Fencer A: step forward to engage in octave.

Fencer B: change the engagement in the low line.

Fencer A: disengage feint into the high line.

Fencer B: parry sixte or quarte.
Fencer A: complete compound attack with lunge or flèche.

★

Fencer B: step forward with a quarte engagement.
Fencer A: change the engagement with a circular action.
Fencer B: change the engagement with either a circular action or lateral pressure.
Fencer A: choose the appropriate indirect attack with lunge or flèche.

★

Fencer A: step and engage quarte, then change to sixte ('double engagement').
Fencer B: cut-over lunge or flèche.
Fencer A: parry high sixte and riposte.

★

Fencer A: engage quarte.
Fencer B: circular change of engagement.
Fencer A: counter-disengage with extension and lunge.
Fencer B: lateral parry followed by direct riposte.
Fencer A: from lunge, parry quarte and counter-riposte direct, by cut-over, disengage, one-two, or detach from the parry and employ a delayed riposte (broken time).

★

Fencer A: step forward with an engagement in quarte or sixte.
Fencer B: circular change of engagement.
Fencer A: counter-disengage with extension (feint).
Fencer B: circular parry.
Fencer A: deceive with a counter-disengagement and lunge or flèche (doublé).

★

Fencer A: from quarte engagement release opponent's blade.
Fencer B: direct lunge and recover with a circular parry.
Fencer A: parry quarte and feint with counter-disengage and extension.
Fencer B: circular parry.
Fencer A: complete the compound riposte with a counter-disengage and flèche.

★

Fencer A: engage sixte.
Fencer B: *either* disengage to absence of blades *or* disengage to absence of blades with a step back.
Fencer A: *either* quarte beat lunge *or* quarte beat feint with half-step then disengage flèche.

★

Fencer A: step forward with a beat and detachment.
Fencer B: step back.
Fencer A: step forward with a through beat in sixte, extending and then immediately retracting the cut-over feint with a half-step (that is, only the front foot is advanced in the step).
Fencer B: parry high sixte and then seconde.
Fencer A: as Fencer B takes seconde, flèche direct.

Part 4: Beyond the Basics

First Intention

Put simply, an attack of first intention is where the fencer has decided to commit to an attack without thought of failure or any secondary action. The fencer has decided on a course of action and is not to be deterred.

Generally speaking there are two approaches to such attacks. They are either the immediate exploitation of an expected action from the opponent, or having manoeuvred the opponent, the launch of a predetermined attack at a moment of the attacker's choosing.

Some of the first type have been considered previously, where the fencer acts promptly on the opportunity afforded by the foot and/or blade action of the opponent to deliver an attack. There is quite a difference between a fencer who, seeing an opening, simply reacts without premeditation and one who expects and is prepared for an opportunity, and can therefore exploit the opportunity at the earliest moment whilst the opponent is unprepared.

The earlier exercises can easily be adapted and combined to serve not simply as mechanical drills or automated responses, but to develop decision making, timing, commitment and speed. The fencer does not attack in every repetition of the exercise, but chooses when to attack, and then moves the point at the earliest possible moment. Practice is needed to ensure that the attack is not telegraphed by premature movement of the body or feet; all actions follow the point in its delivery. The speed of the lunge (although essential) is relegated to secondary importance after the timely, swift and subtle penetration of the point with the fencer remaining very calm at the initiation of the attack.

When retiring, the very action of stopping in order to attack a fencer who is advancing not only signals the intention, but may also trigger an attack from the opponent. The commencement of the attack from retirement, therefore, needs to be disguised. To catch the advancing fencer unprepared in mid-step, do not use a complete step, but step back with the rear foot only (possibly accompanied by some body movement), extend the foil at the moment the rear heel touches the ground and then lunge. Alternatively, at the moment the rear heel touches the ground vigorously extend the arm as the front foot is withdrawn to launch a flèche.

To launch a first intention attack at the moment of the attacker's choosing it is necessary to close to fencing distance and then attack without delay. However, the advance into fencing distance momentarily exposes the fencer, and so this action is best covered with a preparatory blade action such as an engagement or beat. The attack then follows without hesitation.

In delivering a first-intention attack with a step-lunge, the correct coordination of blade and foot is very important. When using a beat followed by a direct attack, the beat should strike a fraction of a second ahead of the rear foot touching the ground as an earlier beat would give the opponent too much time in which to respond. In order to disguise and exploit the correct timing, the beat attack can be introduced with a false blade action during the early part of the step. For example, by indicating an engagement as the front foot advances, the fencer anticipates the automatic blade evasion from the opponent which is then subjected to the beat just as the step is about to be completed.

Conversely, when using a beat to introduce a compound attack, the beat should take place during the advance of the front foot. The step then continues with the feint, allowing time and space for the deception with the lunge.

When using engagements to precede a compound attack, the engagement, like beats, is made early in the step, but for simple

FOIL FENCING

attacks a double-engagement is recommended to occupy and distract the opponent. An engagement, usually of sixte or quarte, is made during the front foot action, and this is immediately followed by a circular change of engagement during the latter part of the step. The hand should progress forward during these actions, levering the opponent's blade by the change of engagement immediately prior to the actual attack by lunge or flèche.

For a successful first intention attack, not only is the appropriate coordination essential, but also the correct cadence. A common error is to start too fast, and not reserve the acceleration until the final action of the attack. By starting too fast or hurrying in the middle of the action the fencer risks losing control of the attack; the initiation of the step and first blade action should be performed almost casually; the second blade action and completion of the step gathers speed, and the full acceleration is reserved for the lunge or flèche.

Exercises

Fencer A: commence a step with an engagement in quarte.
Fencer B: from sixte or quarte guard evade engagement and maintain guard.
Fencer A: complete the step with a circular quarte beat, extension and lunge or flèche.

★

Fencer A: commence a step with an engagement in octave.
Fencer B: from octave, evade engagement and maintain guard.
Fencer A: complete the step with a circular octave beat and lunge to shoulder.
Alternatively, Fencer B evades by lifting the point and Fencer A employs an upward beat (similar to the high sixte position) and disengages to chest.

★

> Fencer A: commence a step with a quarte beat.
> Fencer B: circular change of engagement.
> Fencer A: counter-disengage feint, completing the step.
> Fencer B: circular parry.
> Fencer A: counter-disengage with lunge or flèche.
>
> ★
>
> Fencer A: commence step with engagement in sixte.
> Fencer B: on guard in sixte.
> Fencer A: complete the step with a circular change of engagement and lunge.

Second Intention: Renewals

Renewals of attack or riposte fall into three categories: redouble, remise and reprise. Like the first counter-riposte, they may be performed spontaneously or with second intention to defeat the known response of an adversary.

The Redouble

The redouble is employed against a fencer who parries and hesitates in the parry. Taking advantage of the opponent's momentary hesitation, the attacker relaxes the sword arm and then delivers a second hit by disengage, cut-over or one-two before the opponent can take the initiative. The cut-over and the one-two are the most effective. The redouble by cut-over (see Fig. 30) because the attacker's sword arm drops at the elbow and both blades remain in contact as the original attacker's blade begins to rise, giving the impression of a recovery action (and so helping to maintain a false sense of security within the defender), but it is then completed by a very rapid hit given momentum by the nature of the cut-over. The redouble by one-two is preferable to a simple redouble by disengagement, for if the defender has the ability to parry an attack, then he or she will also have the ability to respond successfully to a simple redouble by disengagement; the one-two exploits this response by deceiving the automatic parry.

Redouble by cut-over.

Fig. 30

Note that it is advisable to follow redoubles with parries so that only one hit is recorded, and thus reduce the possibility of doubt between the priority of a delayed riposte and that of a redouble. It is also in accordance with the objective of hitting without receiving a hit.

Exercise

Fencer A: quarte beat one-two lunge as a false attack.
Fencer B: lateral parry and pause.
Fencer A: cut-over redouble at the commencement of the recovery from lunge.
Fencer B: deliver the delayed riposte with a step forward.
Fencer A: parry the delayed riposte from Fencer B.

The redouble can be practised in a tactical context, but also as a reaction.

*

Progression 1
Fencer B: advance with feint high, feint low, feint high.
Fencer A: retire with quarte riposte, octave riposte, sixte riposte.

Progression 2
Fencer B: advance with feint high, feint low, feint high, but parry the first or second riposte from Fencer A and continue the phrase.
Fencer A: retire with quarte riposte, octave riposte, sixte riposte.

Progression 3
Fencer B: advance with feint high, feint low, feint high, but parry the first or second riposte from Fencer A and continue the phrase or occasionally pause in the parry.
Fencer A: retire with quarte riposte, octave riposte, sixte riposte and redouble when the opportunity arises.

FOIL FENCING

The Remise

When anticipating either a broken time or compound riposte from the opponent, a fencer can employ a remise. Following the opponent's parry, the fencer remains in the original extension of their attack or riposte, and then returns the point to the target as the opponent releases the parry in order to execute a feint or commencement of broken time.

Because a compound or broken-time riposte consists of two or more movements, it is possible to hit the opponent during the execution of their first action and before they commence the final delivery. The remise should be performed with the sword arm extended but relaxed and with no additional redirection of the arm or use of force from the shoulder. Any tension or redirection will usually cause the point to miss the target. Rather, a light insistence from the fingers should be enough for the point to find its target, rebounding back to the original line from the detachment of the defender's parry.

As with redoubles, it is advisable to practise remises followed by parries so that only one hit is recorded. Additionally, the fencer needs to be able to cope with changes of distance, as some fencers tend to step in with their compound ripostes. In this case the fencer executing the remise needs to have the ability to recover from the lunge whilst placing the remise, yet be able to complete the recovery in a guard.

Exercises

Fencer A: feint low, disengage lunge to the opponent's leading shoulder.
Fencer B: successive parries of octave and sixte, followed by detachment with a riposte by one-two (remaining in place).
Fencer A: remain in the extension and remise into the first disengage of Fencer B before recovering to parry the final line of Fencer B's riposte.

★

Fencer A: feint low, disengage lunge to the opponent's leading shoulder.

Fencer B: successive parries of octave and sixte, followed by detachment with a riposte by one-two delivered with a step forward.

Fencer A: during the recovery, remise into the first disengage of Fencer B and complete the recovery, parrying the final line of Fencer B's riposte.

★

Fencer B: engage sixte and cut-over lunge.

Fencer A: parry quarte and riposte direct.

Fencer B: parry quarte remaining on the lunge and riposte by one-two.

Fencer A: remain in the extension and place the remise during the detachment and feint from Fencer B, and then step back out of distance from the final line of the counter-riposte.

The remise is classically a tactical stroke against a compound riposte but it may also be used effectively against a simple riposte provided that the riposte is avoided or parried.

Exercises

Fencer A: beat direct attack.

Fencer B: parry circular sixte and riposte by disengage.

Fencer A: recover with a remise to Fencer B's upper shoulder and a parry of quarte, stepping back.

★

Against a fencer of the opposite handedness:

Fencer A: sixte beat and direct attack.

Fencer B: parry circular sixte and riposte by disengage to upper shoulder.

Fencer A: remise and recover with extension closing out Fencer B's riposte.

Fig. 30

The Reprise

The redouble and the remise are used to renew the offensive against a fencer who maintains or even closes distance. However, in order to continue attacking against a fencer who breaks ground and steps back, the attacker will need an additional foot action together with the renewal of blade action. An attacker who finds themselves short of the target can lever the lunge forward again with a reprise. (See Fig. 31.)

In the lunge the attacker bends the rear knee and advances the rear foot a short distance, then, extending the front leg, pushes vigorously with the rear leg to relaunch the lunge. The body of the fencer should not rise during this action as it offers both an obvious target to the defender and signals the intention of pursuit.

A rising body is usually due to excessive rear foot action. The distance covered by the rear foot is less than that of a recovery forward to guard. In fact the sensation to the fencer as he or she reprises is that of stamping on the same spot with the rear foot. The objective is to rapidly renew the attack over a short distance. For a distance greater than one-third of a blade length, other footwork needs to be employed (reprise with flèche).

Against a defender who parries by detachment and leans or takes a half-step back, a simple direct reprise may suffice, but against a fencer who maintains blade contact, an indirect or compound blade action will be necessary. Indirect blade actions are timed to be launched from the moment that the rear foot strikes the ground, whilst compound blade actions are performed earlier with the feint accompanying the movement of the rear leg, and the final offensive action launched with the renewed lunge.

There are several combinations of footwork that can be used to reprise with a flèche. The rear foot is brought forward and then a vigorous extension from both the rear and front legs launches the flèche. (See Fig. 32.) Alternatively, the rear foot can be brought forward, followed by a slight withdrawal of the front foot before making the final delivery. This permits a change of rhythm and timing, and is suitable for a compound blade action with the feint occurring on the withdrawal of the front foot.

Reprise by flèche (1).

Fig. 32

Reprise by flèche (2).

Fig. 33

Alternatively, withdraw the front foot from the lunge and, with a deeper extension of the sword arm, propel the flèche from the leading leg. (See Fig. 33.) The smooth transition from lunge to flèche, without audible footwork, followed by the rapid conclusion can catch the defender unawares. This flèche from the lunge is also an alternative way of introducing and teaching the flèche as it helps the novice fencer realise the full potential of the extension from toe to weapon tip. When first learning to flèche from on guard, many fencers are premature in passing the rear foot to the front to facilitate a safe landing.

Exercises

Fencer A: step forward with quarte beat direct lunge.
Fencer B: parry quarte and riposte by one-two; sometimes hold the parry and do not riposte.
Fencer A: remise and recover to guard with a parry; if parry is held then redouble by one-two.

⋆

Fencer A: step forward with quarte beat direct lunge.
Fencer B: parry quarte and riposte by one-two; sometimes hold the parry and step back.
Fencer A: remise and recover to guard with a parry; if the parry is held then reprise by lunge or flèche with either an indirect or compound blade action.

⋆

Fencer A: on a detachment from Fencer B, direct lunge.
Fencer B: parry quarte, riposte direct and step back.
Fencer A: on the lunge parry quarte and riposte direct, reprise by lunge or flèche with a one-two compound blade action.

⋆

Fencer B: feint low disengage lunge into the high line.
Fencer A: parry octave sixte and riposte direct.
Fencer B: lateral parry and disengage riposte or recover to guard with the parry.
Fencer A: parry the disengage riposte and step back. If the opponent is seen to recover, then redouble by a flèche with a one-two.

Reprise and Riposte
The reprise may follow a first counter-riposte in order to pursue and renew that offensive against an opponent who gives ground.

However, the opponent may retreat before the commencement of the first counter-riposte, in which case the reprising action can be used to deliver the first counter-riposte itself.

Exercises

Fencer B: engage with circular sixte, parry quarte and riposte direct on Fencer A's attack.
Fencer A: counter-disengage lunge, parry quarte and counter-riposte direct (second intention).
Fencer B: step back with a lateral parry.
Fencer A: reprise by lunge or flèche (withdrawing front foot) with one-two.

*

Fencer B: engage with circular sixte, parry quarte and riposte direct whilst stepping back, complete the recovery to quarte.
Fencer A: counter-disengage lunge, parry quarte; on Fencer B's recovery to quarte *either* deliver the counter-riposte by one-two whilst reprising with a lunge *or* deliver the counter-riposte by disengage and cut-over using a reprise by flèche.

Takings or Prises de Fer

Following the successful completion of a parry it is sometimes advisable to maintain blade contact with the attacker's blade. If, for example, the attacker is prone to remise or redouble then do not release the parried blade or pause in the parry as either course will give the opponent a chance of delivering a renewal. It is better to move continuously (denying the redouble) and maintain blade contact (denying the remise).

This is achieved by a 'taking' of the blade, otherwise known as a 'prise de fer'. Basic prises de fer include those illustrated in Figures 7a and 7b on page 23, as they are formed from the transports shown. However, in forming the transport the hand is advanced, thus levering the opposing blade. They differ from engagements and parries in that they are formed against a blade that is in line (that is, extended in a straight line), and contact is between the opponent's foible and the defender's forte against the shell of the weapon.

Prises de fer are also employed to deliver ripostes in a line not expected by the opponent. For example, if an attack is parried in octave the successful defender can lever the attacker's blade from octave to quarte (against an adversary of the opposite handedness this will expose the back and flank for a riposte). Likewise from a parry of sixte the opponent's blade can be taken to septime or high septime as illustrated in Figure 34.

Bind of septime (two views).

Fig. 34

Binds

An action that transports the opponent's blade diagonally is a 'bind'; it is executed with a slight forward action of the blade as it is transported. It is this forward action that gives the bind its quality of leverage that takes dominance over the opposing weapon and distinguishes it from a transport. Binds may be performed fruitfully from octave to quarte, quarte to octave or seconde, sixte to septime (or high septime), and sixte through septime and then pronating to prime.

An allied action, sometimes referred to as 'the destructive parry', can be very useful. From a quarte guard against an opponent who feints by disengagement: as the disengagement passes from under the hand it is met with a septime parry that is additionally pushed slightly forward and out of line. Performed vigorously and well timed, this action often has the effect of disarming the opponent.

Two established prises de fer that are perhaps more flamboyantly theatrical than practical are (1) from a parry of sixte, binding direct to prime, and (2) from prime binding to sixte or tierce. Both, however, are useful if the intention is to close distance for an angulated hit. The former bind can be used against a fencer of the opposite handedness to introduce a cut-over action from prime to the opponent's chest.

Envelopments

An 'envelopment' may be used as an alternative to a bind. This is where the fencer describes a complete circle from and returning to the original parry or guard. The most common is an envelopment in sixte, as illustrated in Figure 35.

Envelopment.

Fig. 35

Croisé

An action that may be used against a fencer who, from their attack, returns to guard with their blade and arm stiffly extended is a 'croisé'. This involves either lifting or bearing down the opponent's point whilst retaining blade contact on the same side of the body. For example, from a parry of septime either lift the blade to high septime or rotate the hand and blade to the pronated position of prime, simultaneously lifting the opponent's blade and stepping forward. From quarte simultaneously lower the hand and guard (maintaining blade contact and keeping the point raised) whilst carrying the hand outside the line of fencing. The first example enables the fencer to move inside the reach of the opponent, and from within that reach to safely detach from the opposing blade and form a hit with angulation. The second example enables the fencer to conclude a hit by lowering the point and directing an angulated hit at the target below the opponent's sword arm. (See Fig. 36.)

Croisé to flank from quarte parry.

Fig. 36

Exercises

Fencer A: stepping forward quarte beat feint direct.
Fencer B: lateral parry and direct riposte (in place).
Fencer A: parry quarte, form croisé and step forward or lunge to hit.

Against a fencer of the same handedness the point is angulated to hit from outside and below the sword arm. Against a fencer of the opposite handedness the hit has the character of a low opposition hit.

★

Fencer A: stepping forward, quarte beat feint direct.
Fencer B: lateral parry and disengage riposte.
Fencer A: parry quarte-sixte, bind to septime and riposte, *or* bind to high septime *or* bind to septime and then pronate to prime with a step forward and riposte with angulation.

★

Fencer A: stepping forward quarte beat feint direct.
Fencer B: lateral parry and direct riposte (in place).
Fencer A: parry quarte, form croisé and lunge to hit, redouble from flank to shoulder and recover to sixte.

If the fencers are of the same handedness, then sometimes continue as follows:
Fencer B: attempt to parry the croisé by withdrawing to octave (or seconde) and then riposte by disengaging high.
Fencer A: following the attempted redouble, recover to sixte then attempt to bind or envelop the opponent's blade and riposte.

★

Fencer A: engage quarte and change the engagement to sixte. Fencer B: deceive the sixte change of engagement with a disengage lunge to the low target. Fencer A: parry octave with a step back, bind to quarte and riposte *or*, against a fencer of the opposite handedness, bind to quarte, step forward and reverse the blade to prime for an angulated riposte.

*

Fencer A: engage quarte.
Fencer B: disengage and lunge.
Fencer A: parry circular quarte and riposte by disengage or one-two, or against a fencer of the same handedness: bind to octave (this will have a similar effect to a feint and induce the opponent to parry) then disengage riposte to the shoulder.

*

Against a fencer of the opposite handedness:
Fencer A: engage quarte.
Fencer B: disengage and lunge.
Fencer A: parry sixte.
Fencer B: disengage to redouble.
Fencer A: parry octave, lift the opponent's blade (croisé) and riposte to the rear, shoulder or back. If necessary step forward and use angulation or employ a hit with point momentum for the riposte.

Consolidation Exercises

Fencer A: beat extend advancing the front foot.
Fencer B: *either* step back with a circular parry, then take a lateral parry *or* step back with circular parry, then extend blade and arm in line.

Fencer A: *either* counter-disengage in completing the step, followed by a disengage lunge or flèche, *or* counter-disengage in completing the step followed by a quarte parry and croisé to hit with step or lunge.

*

Fencer A: engage sixte with a step forward and on Fencer B's return pressure disengage lunge.

Fencer B: *either* lateral parry followed by one-two compound riposte *or* lateral parry and step back with extension of arm and blade.

Fencer A: on the lunge remise or, if the opponent steps back with a line, recover forward engaging sixte, envelopment in sixte and lunge or flèche.

Defence: Ceding Parries and Defence against Prises de Fer

Because of the nature of a hit delivered by a prise de fer, a fencer, not being able to free the blade, cannot always form a parry in the normal manner from detachment. Instead, it is sometimes necessary to permit the foible to be taken without resistance (cede) and then turn the forte of the blade to oppose the conclusion of the thrust in its final line.

For example, following an opponent's envelopment in the high line or bind from low to high, the defender's blade may be forced aside by a thrust on the sixte side of the blade. The thrust should not be resisted. Instead, whilst lowering the point, the hand is inverted to the pronated position of prime as it is carried across the body. The defender's blade pivots on that of the aggressor, contact is maintained throughout and the attacking blade follows the course of the defender's foil movement to arrive on the forte of the defender. (See Fig. 37.)

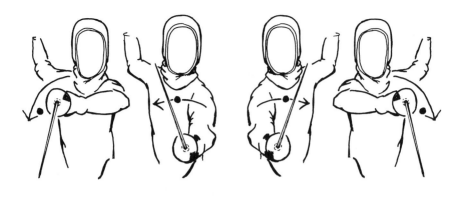

right-hander   Ceding to prime.   left-hander

Fig. 37

A prise de fer that lifts and finishes on the defender's quarte side is relatively easy to parry provided that the defender delays the final opposition of the forte until the attacker's blade is felt on the inside (quarte side) of the blade. (See Fig. 38.)

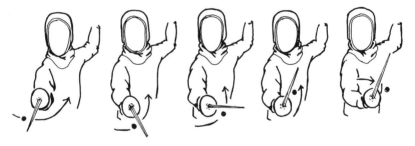

Ceding quarte parry.

Fig. 38

The natural response to resist against the attacking blade has the effect of pushing the attack towards the lower target, with possibly painful results.

Exercises

Assumes two fencers of the same handedness:
Fencer B: engage sixte with a step forward and on Fencer A's return pressure disengage lunge.
Fencer A: lateral parry and step back with extension of arm and blade.
Fencer B: from the lunge recover forward, engaging sixte, envelopment in sixte and lunge or flèche.
Fencer A: cede to prime and riposte by angulation.

★

Fencer A: beat feint direct and counter-disengage lunge.
Fencer B: circular sixte parry on Fencer A's feint followed by a parry of octave, lift blade for riposte by croisé.
Fencer A: recover ceding into quarte and riposte appropriate to the distance.

★

Assumes two fencers of the opposite handedness:
Fencer A: beat disengage feint and counter-disengage lunge.
Fencer B: circular sixte parry on Fencer A's feint followed by a parry of octave, riposte by bind to quarte.
Fencer A: recover ceding into prime and riposte appropriate to the distance.

Against an opponent's quarte croisé: once the defender feels the blade being taken by the force of the croisé, the point is permitted to drop and then, as the thrust advances, the defender rapidly turns to seconde and pushes outwards to oppose and deflect the attacking blade. (See Fig. 39a.) Blade contact is usually maintained throughout the action. The defender should not simply drop the hand to block the attacker, for the attacker can simply lift the point and continue to the then-exposed shoulder. (See Fig. 39b.)

correct

Fig. 39a

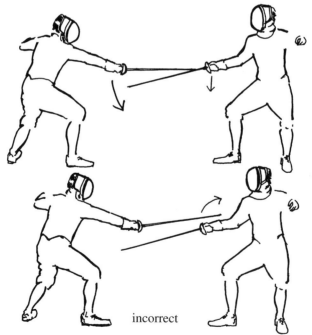

incorrect

Defence against a croisé.

Fig. 39b

Defence: Counter-Offensive Actions

These are hits that are launched into the opponent's offensive action instead of a parry as a defensive action. Some fencers may instinctively respond to a threat in this way; however, such actions are better employed tactically.

The remise into a compound riposte is such an action. Tactically the fencer, anticipating a particular riposte, uses the remise to hit at the moment the adversary commences their action, and well before they can commence the final action of the riposte. The remise as a second intention counter-offensive action on a compound riposte has the advantage that the original attacker has taken the initiative, has a clear extension of the arm and blade, their point has a shorter distance to travel to the target than that of the opponent, and the fencer performing the remise is placed to recover and defend following the remise.

If we contrast this with a fencer who hits into an attack, we can see that none of these advantages are present. Thus a fencer who responds to an attack with a counter-attack (or stop-hit) starts at a disadvantage. This disadvantage may be overcome where there is a noticeable imbalance between the reach, speed, experience and technique of the two fencers. A tall fencer, with fast reactions, good timing and coordination may be able to extend, hit and step away from the poorly executed attack of a novice fencer without receiving a hit. However, the same action against an equal opponent would have little chance of success. If the attacking opponent has already taken the initiative with a simple attack and is in the act of delivering a hit, the defender cannot hope to deliver a timely stop-hit. Even against a compound or broken-time attack, a spontaneous stop-hit is a dangerous stroke liable to failure. It may be possible for a fencer to perceive the commencement of a broken-time or compound attack launched at him or her, but if the stop-hit is a spontaneous reaction then it will still be unable to arrive ahead of the commencement of the attacker's final delivery. The best that can be expected of such a stop-hit is that it will arrive simultaneously with the attack, and in that case, the initiative and priority being with the attacker, they alone will be awarded the hit.

To successfully deliver a counter-attack it is necessary to remember the guiding principle: 'to hit without being hit'. It may be possible to achieve this because of the physical differences between the fencers, but otherwise it will require body evasion, opposition of the blade, tactical application, or a combination of the same. In Figure 40, the right fencer commences an attack delivered from their sixte line; the left fencer, in expectation of this attack, moves his hand and blade to the quarte side, thrusting in opposition, and simultaneously moving the rear foot out of line and turning the left shoulder in order to protect the target. (See Fig. 40.)

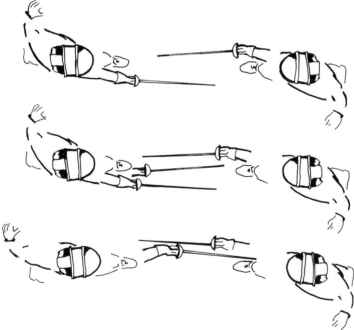

A stop-hit in quarte opposition with foot and body displacement.

Fig. 40

The fencer who chooses to counter-attack is advised to maintain the initiative by inducing the opponent to attack so that the counter-attack takes the place of a premeditated parry rather than being formed as an instinctive response to a threat.

Exercises

Fencer A: half-step forward with a circular engagement of sixte.
Fencer B: counter-disengage lunge.
Fencer A: quarte opposition thrust completing the step with body displacement and the rear foot out of line.

★

Fencer A: half-step forward with a circular engagement of sixte.
Fencer B: counter-disengage lunge.
Fencer A: complete the step forward into a squat position with the hand and blade thrust high in the sixte line. The hand should be higher than the mask at the completion of the action. (See Fig. 41.)

Duck stop-hit.

Fig. 41

A fencer having suffered a hit, or series of hits, delivered by compound or broken-time attacks will be able to avoid a repetition by subsequently giving ground, with or without additional parries. However, this fails to score and leaves the opponent with the initiative. The tactical answer to such attacks is not to parry them, but to counter-attack them in such a way that they fail to arrive, usually by anticipating and closing the final line of the attack.

Exercises

Fencer A: engage with circular sixte.

Fencer B: change engagement to quarte.

Fencer A: give pressure to trigger Fencer B's compound attack by one-two.

Fencer B: one-two compound attack with a lunge.

Fencer A: half form the parry of sixte, but instead of completing the sixte parry and subsequent quarte parry, direct the point in an arc to septime simultaneous with a thrust of the hand at shoulder height (and possibly body evasion by removing the rear foot out of line). The effect is a stop-hit in opposition against the final line of the compound attack.

*

Fencer B: step forward with feint of cut-over.

Fencer A: step back with feint of high sixte parry.

Fencer B: step with feint low and lunge to the high line.

Fencer A: thrust the hand and blade in the line of sixte, opposing and closing out Fencer B's final line of attack with a stop-hit. (See Fig. 42.)

A stop-hit in opposition or 'time thrust'.

Fig. 42

Part 5: Additional Combat Skills

Close-Quarter Fencing

The techniques employed by the fencer change with the distance between the adversaries. When fencing at close quarters, there is greater use of pronated hand positions and hits with angulation. There are several situations that give rise to close-quarter fencing: (1) the opponent attacks, ripostes or renews with a flèche; (2) the opponent, having failed in an initial attack, tries to force the attack through; or (3) a defender deliberately closes the distance after a parry in order to move inside the opponent's reach.

From the quarte parry there is no time, with the rapid closing of targets, to extend the blade and arm for a riposte against a flèche. Instead, the hand remains in the quarte parry, moves away from the body and slightly back as the point is lowered into the oncoming target directed by the fingers. The angle formed to make this riposte is not held rigidly but is more like a flick. Alternatively, from the parry of quarte the hand is raised, detaching from the opponent's blade, and the defender's blade is inverted to a prime position at a height at least level with the head. (See Fig. 43.) During the inversion of the blade, the point is taken back in an arc from high to low. Speed comes from the momentum of the point which should strike the opponent as the bodies draw level. This stroke is especially effective against someone of the opposite handedness.

Riposte from quarte using inversion through prime.

Fig. 43

Again, from the sixte parry there is no time to extend for the riposte against a flèche. Instead, the hand can be pronated to tierce and moved out and/or back to give greater security whilst forming an angle to facilitate a riposte. Alternatively, a riposte through the high position of prime may be used as before and is especially useful against someone of the opposite handedness.

Against a flèche parried in high septime it is only necessary to rotate the hand to pronation whilst taking it back to form the prime-like hit previously described. However, it is necessary to draw the point back as the hand rotates in order to direct it forward again with a flick-like action to the oncoming target.

To practise the final angle of this particular angulated hit, place the point with the hand in supination, arm extended, on a target at chest height, and then walk towards the target. Turn the hand to pronation as if reading the time on a wrist watch (on the back of the wrist!) and carry the hand over the quarte shoulder, slightly above head height; the point remains lightly fixed on the target. Next, place the point on the chest of a training partner who then walks towards you. Using the same movement, keep the point fixed. Later, practise stepping forward from sixte or quarte to deliver this hit, or have a training partner step towards you.

Against a fencer who, having been parried, tends to continue forward, turn the successful parry from the supinated hand position into its corresponding pronated hand position. This achieves three things: (1) the pronated hand position is much firmer than the supinated hand position because the hand and forearm are directly opposed to the opponent's blade; (2) the alignment of hand and forearm makes it easier to push the opponent's blade further out of line; and (3) the pronation facilitates the use of angulated ripostes at the closer distance.

The hand actions are those shown earlier in Figure 17 on page 53. From the parry of sixte turn to tierce, from octave to seconde and from septime to prime. (See Fig. 44.) Additionally, from the parry of high septime pronate so that the knuckles are uppermost (similar to the sabre parry of quinte).

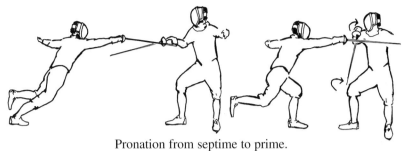

Pronation from septime to prime.

Fig. 44

A fencer who tends to lean or fall forward at the end of the attack exposes very little immediate target. However, the back is vulnerable if a successful defender knows how to exploit the situation. From the parry, with a step or half-step forward if necessary, the hand is thrown somewhat higher than normal for the riposte; the point describes a rapid arc to the target and the necessary angulation is achieved because of the momentum of the point.

In Figure 45 the blade is taken in an arc from a parry of septime, initially moving to the rear but being delivered with almost the quality of a cut-over having passed through the position of prime.

A riposte to the back.

Fig. 45

Likewise the position of prime could be held as the defender steps forward inside the reach of the opponent and then ripostes. In dealing with a fencer of the opposite handedness, a parry of prime can be taken against the adversary's quarte riposte. From this dominant position a number of riposting actions are available.

In Figure 46 the attacker has been parried in quarte, but, by rotating the hand, can cede into a parry of prime (see Fig. 46a) to prevent the direct riposte.

Fig. 46

Fig. 46a

Fig. 46b

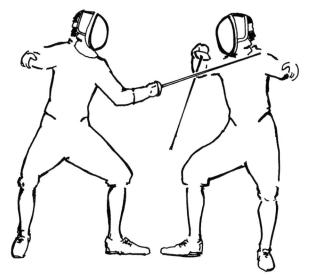

Fig. 46c

Options for the counter-riposte include an immediate flicking or throwing of the point to the target whilst maintaining the prime hand position (with or without a recovery forward), or from a short pause as the opponent begins to recover in their sixte line and resist the blade contact in prime, a cut-over action as an indirect riposte. (See Fig. 46b.) This latter action may be accompanied with a closing of distance.

Alternatively, the parry of prime can be held as the distance is closed (see Fig. 46c) and the riposte delivered with a disengage to chest, or with a one-two compound riposte. More effectively, by detaching from the parry when safely inside the opponent's reach, a riposte to the back with angulation – the hand taking the profile of tierce – finishes the action.

Another useful close-quarter stroke against a fencer of the opposite handedness is from a parry of octave. The distance is closed as the blade is lifted (croisé) in order to score on the opponent's exposed back.

When a fencer suddenly finds themselves at close quarters they should not step back. Doing so gives the opponent the opportunity to hit because the retiring fencer, in opening the distance, gives an easier target whilst delaying their blade action. For example, in a parry of quarte when the opponent's lunge has finished too close, a step back would give the time and target for the attacker to redouble. Rather the immediate response should be to attempt an angulated hit or step forward; the closer the fencer to the opponent the safer, as the weapons cannot be wielded. (See Fig. 47.)

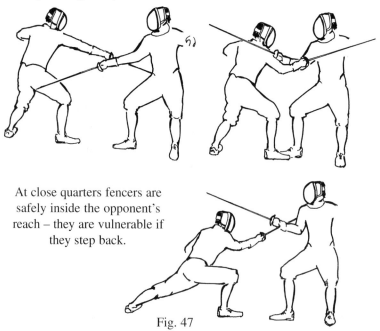

At close quarters fencers are safely inside the opponent's reach – they are vulnerable if they step back.

Fig. 47

Even at the closest of distances it is often still possible to move and free the blade to hit. The simple expedient of passing the rear foot forward and pivoting on the sole of the front foot, will safely bring the fencer alongside the opponent. The hand is dropped to a low tierce and an angulated hit delivered. (See Fig. 48.)

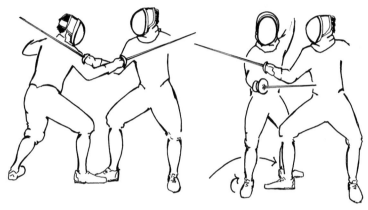

Fig. 48

Accelerating the Hit

In the last section we saw that for some hits we rely on 'the momentum of the point'. The point of a modern fencing weapon has a greater potential for speed than the hand controlling it. This is because the blade has a degree of flexibility and is weighted by the scoring button. An authentic combat weapon has neither of these characteristics and was designed for penetration. The sports weapon needs only to touch.

Fencing, even a few decades ago, was largely taught on the basis of the 'correctness' of the thrust without due regard for the differences of the modern weapon. These differences enable the modern point to be 'thrown', giving far greater speed than before. Previously I have referred to the nature of a hit as sometimes having the characteristics of a cut-over, as arc-like, or being like a flick. A hitting action that starts from the fingers and hand to throw the point to the target will result in a faster blade action and earlier hit than a blade that is simply propelled towards the opponent by a forward action of the arm alone. (See Fig. 49.)

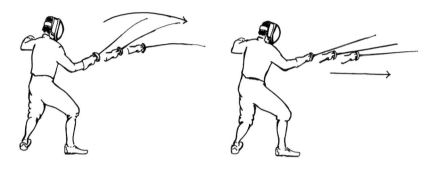

Fig. 49

Additionally, because the point is thrown towards the target, it can fix on a target that is oblique to the attacker whereas a blade thrust in a straight line may graze such a target without fixing, and a hit that is attempted by extending the arm prior to using the hand to direct the point will result in the blade landing flat as a slap, and again the point will not fix. (See Fig. 50.)

correct

incorrect

incorrect

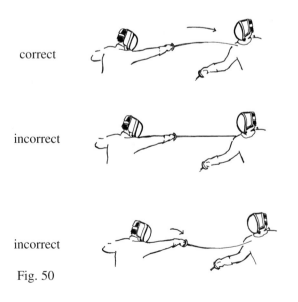

Fig. 50

A riposte delivered in this thrown manner from a premeditated high line parry can be particularly effective if directed to the opponent's shoulder, either high or over the shoulder to the rear.

The hit with point momentum (coup lancé) is sometimes referred to as a 'flick hit', but this is a misnomer. Such a name implies that the hand may approach the target in order to carry out a short, sharp action; it also implies a snatching away from the target. However, it is critical that the point must start moving very early in the action of hitting and be directed so that its momentum causes it to fix on the target.

Second Intention: Counter-Time

Counter-time is the commencement of an attack in order to induce a counter-attack which can then be parried in order to score with a riposte. It is one possible tactical response to a fencer who employs stop-hits. The alternative is to take the initiative with a simple attack so that the stop-hit arrives too late to score. However, this second choice is not always available if, for example, the opponent has a superior reach or causes the attack to miss. Also, in the case of both fencers hitting, it is not always clear which fencer has priority and it is, therefore, desirable to ensure that only one hit is clearly registered.

Exercises

Fencer A: step forward with quarte beat feint direct.
Fencer B: extend direct (stop-hit) with body evasion.
Fencer A: parry quarte and riposte by croisé, employing angulation and point momentum.

*

Fencer A: step forward with a sixte or quarte beat and feint low.
Fencer B: extend direct (stop-hit) in the high line whilst stepping back.

Fencer A: *either* parry sixte, envelop and lunge, exploiting the point momentum *or* parry sixte, bind to septime and lunge or flèche.

★

Fencer A: engage in sixte.

Fencer B: give pressure to trigger Fencer A's compound attack by one-two.

Fencer A: disengage feint only (do not complete the one-two).

Fencer B: extend direct.

Fencer A: parry with prime and step forward to riposte at close quarters.

★

Fencer B: quarte beat followed by lunge to the target below the opponent's sword arm, recover to sixte and step back.

Fencer A: parry octave, pause and then on Fencer B's completion of recovery step (or half-step) with feint of cut-over or broken time.

Fencer B: extend direct for a stop-hit.

Fencer A: parry quarte and riposte by croisé to flank, *or* by bind to octave *or* by flèche direct.

★

Fencer A: sixte through beat, feint of cut-over with half-step or step.

Fencer B: extend direct.

Fencer A: beat-like quarte parry and riposte with flèche. (See Fig. 51.)

Counter-time.

Fig. 51

Defence: Parries – Reaction, Premeditation and Inducement

When training, the fencer needs to practise the formation of a parry under three different conditions: (1) as a reaction to an

129

attack or riposte; (2) as a reaction to the deception of an initial parry; and (3) as a tactical stroke.

In all cases it is imperative that the fencer does not overreact and take unnecessarily exaggerated parries, reducing the opportunity of either a successful riposte or of a subsequent parry. Nor should the hand be allowed to withdraw towards the body whilst forming a parry, but rather the fencer should withdraw with footwork. Conditioning with linked transports as in Part 1, and developing transports from sixte and circular sixte to high sixte, and from there to seconde are necessary prerequisites to developing control of parries and successive parries.

To deal with attacks successfully it is first necessary to become inured to feints and to have the ability to maintain correct fencing distance. If the opponent is permitted inside this distance then defence becomes more difficult. To react defensively to a feint or loss of distance is to signal the intention of the parry and give the opponent the chance to deceive it or to plan a later attack. The parry should be executed late in the attack, giving the attacker little or no time to respond and therefore making them vulnerable to a riposte.

Exercises

Fencer A: engaged in quarte.
Fencer B: disengage feint *or* disengage lunge.
Fencer A: ignore any feint, on the lunge from Fencer B step back with a circular parry of quarte and riposte.

*

Fencer B: from mobility engage quarte and *either* step forward, maintaining the engagement *or* step forward with a feint direct before retiring.
Fencer A: on any of the above actions step back on guard, maintaining distance and without any blade response to Fencer B's preparation or feint.

Fencer B: occasionally from the quarte engagement, step with a feint direct followed by a lunge or flèche direct.

Fencer A: on the attacking action only continue to retire and parry as late as possible; riposte as appropriate.

In dealing with the deception of a parry, the defender will need to take two or more parries (successive parries) in order to deflect the compound or broken-time attack. Automatic defensive systems can be perfected based on the transports; for example, from a guard in sixte take a parry of quarte followed by a circular parry of quarte (or semicircular septime), or, again from sixte, take a parry of high sixte followed by a seconde parry.

In building such defensive systems it is first necessary to practise the appropriate sequence of transports by transporting the partner's or coach's blade and checking the correct formation of each position. In subsequent practice the coach partner should free the blade immediately on the completion of each transport or after a short delay to permit the next transport. Later the coach partner should free the blade during one of the transports and later still deceive such a transport completely. By using the feel of the blade and variations of timings, the fencer becomes conditioned to pausing when a parry is successful and responding with a further appropriate and controlled parry when necessary, either against a redouble or a compound attack.

Exercises

Progression 1
Fencer B: step with feint direct.
Fencer A: step back with a quarte parry.
Fencer B: redouble with disengage and step.
Fencer A: step back circular quarte parry and riposte.

Progression 2
Fencer B: step with feint direct and stop *or* deceive Fencer A's parry of quarte and lunge.

Fencer A: step back with a quarte parry *or* step back with a parry of quarte followed by a circular parry of the compound attack.

Progression 3
Fencer B: step forward with feint *or* feint and redouble *or* compound attack.
Fencer A: step back with parry of quarte and take a further circular parry of quarte as necessary.

★

Fencer B: engage Fencer A's sixte line and, on the return pressure, disengage step with a feint.
Fencer A: quarte riposte and step back on guard in quarte.
Fencer B: quarte counter-riposte direct with a step *or* by disengage and step.
Fencer A: from quarte take a circular parry of quarte (and riposte) against the disengage counter-riposte.

★

Fencer A: engage sixte and disengage lunge, recover to quarte and step back.
Fencer B: lateral parry and riposte by disengage lunge on Fencer A's recovery *or* direct riposte in place followed by a redouble by disengage with a lunge.
Fencer A: circular parry of quarte.

★

Progression 1
Fencer B: from Fencer A's sixte engagement disengage feint with step.
Fencer A: step back with circular sixte parry.
Fencer B: step forward with disengage redouble.
Fencer A: step back with parry of high sixte.
Fencer B: redouble by lunge with disengage to flank.
Fencer A: parry seconde and riposte.

Progression 2
Fencer B: from Fencer A's sixte engagement, disengage feint with step.
Fencer A: step back with circular sixte parry.
Fencer B: deceive Fencer A's circular parry with a counter-disengage *or* cut-over and lunge.
Fencer A: step back with parry of high septime.
Fencer B: redouble to flank.
Fencer A: parry seconde and riposte to back using point momentum.

Progression 3
Fencer B: from Fencer A's sixte engagement, disengage feint with step, deceive both the circular and high septime parries and lunge to flank.
Fencer A: stepping back, take circular sixte, high septime and seconde parry and riposte.

Unlike other parries where the fencer learns to respond safely against the adversary's initiative, the tactical parry puts the fencer in control of the opponent's offensive action. Tactical parries include a second-intention first counter-riposte and counter-time, but they also include inducements for the opponent to attack (sometimes referred to as 'invitations' although they should not be as obvious as the name would suggest!). For example, following a short series of changes of engagement, pause momentarily and any attack into the open line can be met with a premeditated parry. Another example is when, from shallow quarte engagement, a disengage feint from the opponent is immediately intercepted with a destructive parry of septime.

Otherwise, against a fencer who uses feints, repeatedly step out of distance but, when ready, quickly half form a parry (feint-parry) to trigger the final attack into a prepared defence. Ideally take the feint-parry during the rear foot withdrawal of the step so that the final parry is formed as the step is completed with the front foot. The riposte can then be delivered in place or as the rear foot commences the next step away from the attacker. Against a fencer who advances with feints of cut-over or with the point high, a feint-parry of high sixte can induce the final line of the attack under the defender's hand and into a firm seconde parry and riposte. However, against a fencer who, whilst advancing, uses multiple feints below the hand, a through beat parry of septime can be employed at a moment of the defender's choosing. On other occasions a feint of stop-hit might be appropriate.

Against a fencer who advances and prepares with shallow high line engagements or uses grazes seeking to attack by disengagement or counter-disengagement, take a feint half-parry of octave or septime instead of responding with a lateral or circular change of engagement as expected. The aggressor is denied their chosen route under the hand, and if they attack it will be into a high line and a premeditated quarte (or sixte) parry and riposte can be effected.

A simple practice manoeuvre is for the fencer to advance and engage in either sixte or quarte and for the partner to disengage attack. The fencer then parries with a circle in quarte or sixte as appropriate and ripostes. In this case the fencer is not reacting to an unknown situation, but learning that they have choice and initiative and can control an attack.

One further opportunity to exploit is as the opponent attempts to renew a failed attack. Having successfully parried an initial attack, instead of riposting immediately, step back, maintaining the parry and as the opponent attempts to redouble or reprise, meet them with a further parry that immediately introduces the riposte. The advantage of this timing is that it often overextends the original attacker who is reacting in a spontaneous but predictable manner.

Parries that tactically anticipate and intercept the opponent's offence are very often performed with a beat-like action allowing the riposte to 'ricochet' to the target.

To summarise, there are only four groups of offensive actions that pose a threat, and the use of the parry and riposte in a controlled tactical manner to take the initiative from the opponent can be introduced in one of two ways: either a feint, or an inducement to draw the action that is to be parried. The appropriate actions are:

1) to deal with attacks, induce then parry and riposte.
2) to deal with counter-attacks, feint then parry and riposte.
3) to deal with ripostes, feint then parry and counter-riposte.
4) to deal with renewals, induce and then parry and riposte.

Exercises

Progression 1
Fencer A: step forward with engagement in quarte (on the front foot action).
Fencer B: step back, evading the engagement in the high line.
Fencer A: step back.

Progression 2
Fencer A: step forward with engagement in quarte (on the front foot action).
Fencer B: disengage lunge to chest.
Fencer A: premeditated circular quarte parry (on the completion of the step) and riposte. The quarte parry can be accelerated and the riposte concluded with point momentum.
Alternatively, the final riposte can be delivered in quarte opposition, or, against a fencer of the opposite handedness, the parry can be held during a step forward and the hit delivered by angulation with an inversion to prime.

*

Fencer B: step with an engagement in quarte and advance.
Fencer A: step back, maintaining distance, circular change of engagement with a shallow blade action to trigger Fencer B's compound attack.

Fencer B: step-lunge with compound attack of counter-disengage and disengage.

Fencer A: a shallow lateral parry (feint-parry) followed by final parry and riposte.

(A premeditated counter-attack in opposition can be substituted for the final parry.)

★

Fencer B: advance with blade preparation (for example, engagement, double engagement, engagement and beat, engagement and detachment).

Fencer A: step back in octave to trigger opponent's compound attack.

Fencer B: feint direct and disengage lunge.

Fencer A: feint-parry of quarte followed by final parry and riposte.

(A premeditated counter-attack in opposition can be substituted for the final parry.)

★

Fencer A: step and half-step with engagement in quarte but with hand higher and

further forward than normal. (This denies the opponent the opportunity to disengage above Fencer A's sword arm and exposes the flank.)

Fencer B: lunge to Fencer A's flank.

Fencer A: parry of seconde and riposte as appropriate.

★

Fencer B: beat disengage lunge.

Fencer A: parry sixte with a step back and pause (to induce a redouble).

Fencer B: disengage redouble.

Fencer A: parry octave and riposte with bind, croisé or by detachment.

★

Fencer B: advance.

Fencer A: step back with beat feint direct.

Fencer B: step with circular engagement.

Fencer A: evade with blade in line (feint of dérobement).

Fencer B: parry quarte and riposte with croisé.

Fencer A: premeditated parry of seconde and riposte as appropriate.

The Dérobement

The conventions of foil fencing respect the initiative and priority taken by a fencer. Earlier we saw that there are difficulties in delivering counter-attacks and one reason for this is that the attacker has taken the initiative and the counter-attacker is only responding. The difficulty is compounded by the not infrequent difficulty in judging fencing time. I stated that it may be possible for a fencer to perceive the commencement of a broken-time or compound attack but be unable to hit clearly ahead of the commencement of the attacker's final delivery. There is, however, one stroke that permits the fencer to take the initiative against an enthusiastic and animated aggressor: the line and dérobement.

By starting with the arm extended and the blade in line, threatening the target, priority is given to the fencer 'in line' and the other fencer is required first to remove (or avoid) the line in order to take an offensive action.

The dérobement is the evasion of the opponent's attempt to take the blade. For example, Fencer A stands with his or her blade in line, and Fencer B advances rapidly with an engagement of sixte and direct lunge. Fencer A, retaining the line, times a small disengagement so that Fencer B misses the blade and the momentum of Fencer B's lunge or flèche causes impalement on the blade in line. (See Fig. 52.)

Fencer B   Fencer A

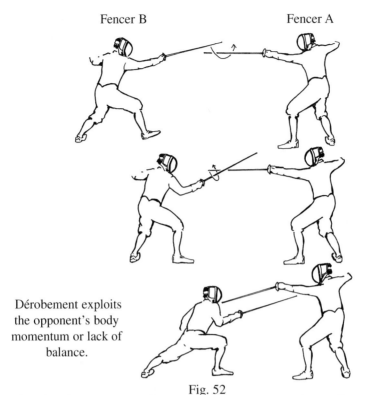

Dérobement exploits
the opponent's body
momentum or lack of
balance.

Fig. 52

The dérobement may be simple or compound, evading one or more attempts to take the blade. (See Fig. 53.)

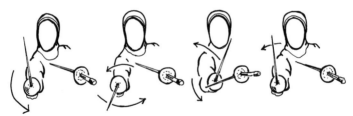

Simple dérobement against a circular sixte engagement.

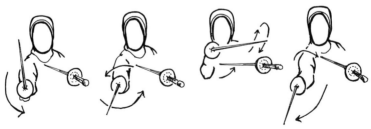

Compound dérobement against high followed by seconde.

Fig. 53

However, an opponent is not likely to be fooled into lunging or flèching onto a point in line from a static position or obvious presentation of the blade. They are more likely to respond spontaneously during a phrase in the bout, but this can lead to the same problem as with counter-attacks, namely, that at speed and from mobility, it is not always possible for the initial offensive action (in this case the line) to be correctly identified. The simple solution is to precede the giving of the line with an action on the opposing blade. This has the dual advantage of clearly establishing the initiative whilst at the same time triggering the anticipated blade preparation from the opponent.

Exercises

Fencer A: step forward from sixte to octave, then take two steps back in sixte.

Fencer B: in sixte, step back and then advance on Fencer A's retirement.

Fencer A: quarte beat extend in line as Fencer B advances.

Fencer B: on receiving the line, immediately take a sixte circular parry and lunge or flèche direct.

Fencer A: maintaining the point in line, deceive (dérobe) the sixte parry.

*

Fencer B: advance in the low line.

Fencer A: septime beat feint direct in the high line.

Fencer B: parry high septime, parry seconde and riposte high whilst advancing.

Fencer A: maintain the line, deceiving the parries.

*

Fencer B: beat, counter-disengage and lunge.

Fencer A: step back with a circular sixte parry, followed by a quarte parry, detach and step back giving a line (in place of riposte).

Fencer B: recover forward, taking circular sixte and lunge.

Fencer A: dérobe.

Part 6: Tactical Applications

With such a wealth of choice of actions available to the fencer it is sometimes difficult to choose the most appropriate stroke for a given situation. Some fencers may be especially talented with a particular action or tactic, but when their favourite stroke fails, they are at a loss to find an alternative effective stroke. Other fencers may repeat strokes fruitlessly simply because of a lack of ideas under the pressure of combat. Yet others may unnecessarily complicate a stroke to overcome the opponent's defence or become mesmerised by the complexity of their opponent's blade work.

Whatever the reason, it is beneficial to categorise the many fencing actions into their component groups to simplify the process of tactical analysis and application. There are two simplified schematics based on such categorisation. They are independent, but at the same time not mutually exclusive.

The Square

In the first and simplest schematic, all offensive actions are grouped into three primary categories and one secondary category. The primary offensive actions are attack, counter-attack and riposte. The secondary offensive actions are the renewals (remise, redouble and reprise). From this, a simple tactical schematic, or game plan can be devised.

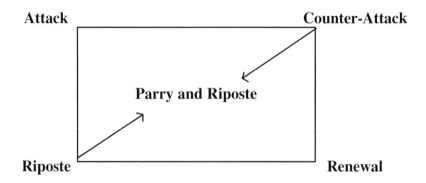

In this schematic:

• If an attack fails because it is countered by a successful riposte or counter-attack, then, rather than complicate subsequent attacks, the tactical response is a second intention action finishing with a riposte (that is, a first counter-riposte or counter-time).

• If an attack fails because it is countered by an unsuccessful (or badly executed or badly timed) riposte or counter-attack, then the correct tactical response is to employ the same attack followed by a second intention renewal, ignoring the opponent's attempt to riposte or counter-attack.

Exercises

Progression 1
Fencer A: counter-disengage lunge.
Fencer B: quarte parry and riposte direct.

Progression 2
Fencer A: counter-disengage lunge as a false attack.
Fencer B: quarte parry and riposte direct.
Fencer A: second intention parry of quarte and counter-riposte as appropriate.

*

Progression 1
Fencer A: engage sixte and lunge by cut-over.
Fencer B: parry high sixte and riposte to flank.

Progression 2
Fencer A: engage sixte and lunge by cut-over as a false attack.
Fencer B: parry high sixte and riposte to flank.
Fencer A: second intention parry of seconde and riposte as appropriate *or* riposte with step or flèche as appropriate to distance.

*

Fencer A: advance with multiple feints below the opponent's guard.

Fencer B: through-beat of septime and riposte high.

Fencer A: parry high sixte (second intention) and riposte as appropriate.

*

Progression 1

Fencer A: quarte beat feint low and lunge high.

Fencer B: parry octave (or octave then sixte).

Progression 2

Fencer A: quarte beat feint low and lunge high.

Fencer B: opposition stop-hit in sixte.

Progression 3

Fencer A: quarte beat and commence the disengagement of the point.

Fencer B: stop-hit in sixte.

Fencer A: parry high sixte (or high septime) and riposte (counter-time).

*

Progression 1

Fencer A: advance with double engagement quarte-sixte, cut-over then lunge with broken time or compound one-two.

Fencer B: on Fencer A's cut-over, stop-hit with body displacement.

Progression 2

Fencer A: advance with double engagement quarte-sixte, cut-over then pause or complete only a half-step.

Fencer B: on Fencer A's cut-over, stop-hit with body displacement.
Fencer A: parry the stop-hit with quarte and riposte by croisé to flank (counter-time).

*

Progression 1
Fencer A: feint of cut-over with a step, direct lunge.
Fencer B: parry quarte with detachment and step back.
Fencer A: recovers.

Progression 2
Fencer A: feint of cut-over with a step, direct lunge.
Fencer B: parry quarte with detachment and step back.
Fencer A: from lunge launch reprise by flèche on Fencer B's detachment.

*

Progression 1
Fencer A: beat direct lunge.
Fencer B: parry quarte and step forward with detachment.

Progression 2
Fencer A: beat direct lunge.
Fencer B: parry quarte and step forward with detachment.
Fencer A: second intention remise with ducking action.

*

Progression 1
Fencer A: engage sixte and lunge by one-two.
Fencer B: successive parries, step forward with feint of one-two or step forward with broken time.
Fencer A: either recover and retire out of distance, or better, recover forward.

Progression 2
Fencer A: engage sixte and lunge by one-two.
Fencer B: successive parries, step forward with feint of one-two or step forward with broken time.
Fencer A: second intention remise.

Note that some fencers, in their eagerness to score a riposte, will advance prematurely and so close the distance unnecessarily. It is only the recovery of the original attacker that permits the time and space for the riposte to have any success. Should the original attacker remain in the lunge or only partially recover, then the riposte may miss or land flat and not register.

*

Progression 1
Fencer A: engage quarte and lunge with disengage to the low target.
Fencer B: extend in octave (causing the attack to miss).

Progression 2
Fencer A: engage quarte and lunge with disengage low and then redouble to the high target from Fencer B's octave extension.

*

Progression 1
Fencer A: step with beat feint of cut-over and broken-time lunge.
Fencer B: on Fencer A's cut-over, extend for a stop-hit and retire on guard.

Progression 2
Fencer A: step with beat feint of cut-over and half-step.
Fencer B: extend for stop-hit and step back on guard.
Fencer A: on Fencer B's retirement (to guard) launch flèche from half-step.

The Circle

The second tactical schematic, illustrated by the circle below, is more comprehensive than the first schematic and categorises actions into simple offensive, parry and riposte, compound offensive and counter-offensive action. It relies on the relationship between simple and compound offensive actions and defence against them.

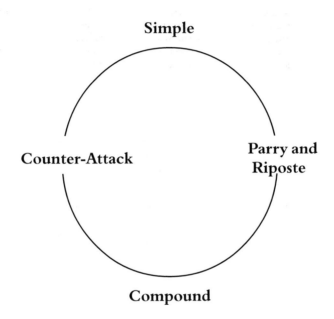

In this schematic we see that the tactical answer to a simple attack is a parry and riposte. If a fencer was previously attempting a counter-attack or was trying to attack on the opponent's preparation of attack but not succeeding, then it is necessary to change from offence to defence. The reality is that the attack is succeeding, and it is poor tactical appreciation to continue with a failing stroke in the endeavour to make it work. Remember that in a bout it is often possible to see an action of preparation but not be quick enough to respond ahead of the opponent's final delivery (especially when the opponent is advancing with a preparation and attack). This is not always easy to accept in the heat of the moment, and, instead of acknowledging the judgement that the attack has been given priority, some fencers will insist on their appreciation of timing. A cool head recognises the reality: the attack needs to be dealt with. On the sighting of whatever action spurred the previous response, this response now becomes a parry in the appropriate line. At the highest level a fencer may even give a feint of their earlier instinctive action in order to draw the attack into a parry.

Taking the schematic further, it is plain that an attack that fails because it is parried can subsequently be adapted to evade the known parry with a compound attack. Using successive parries against the adversary's successful compound attack leaves too much initiative with the attacker. If the compound attack has been achieving success, then clearly the attacker has control of the distance, stroke, and timing of the defender. The tactical response is to thrust against the compound attack with a counter-attack, denying the attacker control of distance and timing, and causing the compound attack to miss whilst at the same time scoring with the counter-attack.

As a guide, any high line compound attack that finishes by disengage in the high line can be countered by a thrust in the low line on the side of the final feint. A high line compound attack that finishes by counter-disengage can be countered by a thrust in the low line on the opposite side to that of the final feint. The effect of this is to thrust into and deflect the attacker's final disengaging action.

In order to gain greater tactical control and timing, the defender can sometimes seek to induce a compound attack. For example, to defeat a fencer who advances from engagement in quarte and attacks by one-two: on the aggressor's engagement step back and give a pressure on the blade to trigger the one-two. From the pressure, immediately thrust in octave to counter-attack and close out the final disengage of the attacker.

Ideally the counter-offensive should score, but even if it does not, it will break up the compound attack so that the original attacker cannot rely on it, and the attacker will, therefore, have to seek alternative strokes and lose the initiative.

Now we come to dealing with the counter-attack. The simplest course of action to defeat the counter-attack is to deliver a simple attack. If broken-time or compound attacks have been thwarted by counter-attacks then it is pointless to use such complex actions. When a fencer initiates a simple attack, the rules of foil (and also of sabre) give him or her priority over the opponent. So, although in historical combat it would be foolhardy to lunge knowing that the antagonist will hit, in the convention of modern fencing we can afford to receive a hit provided that we ourselves do not miss!

The tactical circle, like the tactical square, is not intended as an absolute or complete guide to fencing tactics, but it serves to build comprehension and is a key to simple decision making in a bout. In the case of compound attacks that consist of multiple feints in the low lines or multiple cut-over feints it is better to rely on a feint-parry followed by a parry or stop-hit in opposition.

The same circle can also be applied to deal with ripostes:

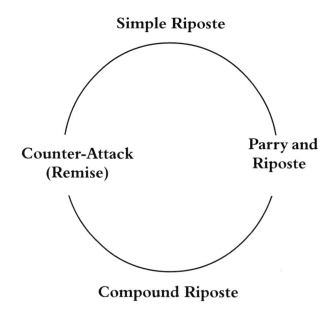

Simple Riposte

Counter-Attack (Remise)

Parry and Riposte

Compound Riposte

In order to overcome successful simple ripostes it is necessary to deflect them, and the tactical response would be a first counter-riposte. In turn, the answer to a fencer who successfully employs counter-ripostes is a compound riposte, and a fencer who employs compound ripostes may be defeated by a remise, which in turn would be nullified by using simple ripostes. Having identified the opponent's tactic, all that is required is to enter the circle at the point of the following action.

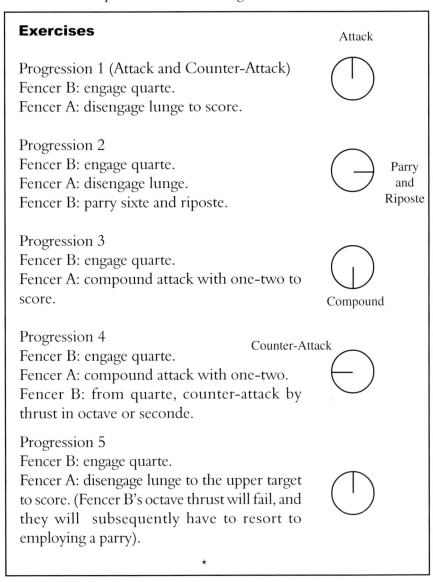

Exercises

Attack

Progression 1 (Attack and Counter-Attack)
Fencer B: engage quarte.
Fencer A: disengage lunge to score.

Progression 2
Fencer B: engage quarte.
Fencer A: disengage lunge.
Fencer B: parry sixte and riposte.

Parry
and
Riposte

Progression 3
Fencer B: engage quarte.
Fencer A: compound attack with one-two to score.

Compound

Progression 4
Counter-Attack
Fencer B: engage quarte.
Fencer A: compound attack with one-two.
Fencer B: from quarte, counter-attack by thrust in octave or seconde.

Progression 5
Fencer B: engage quarte.
Fencer A: disengage lunge to the upper target to score. (Fencer B's octave thrust will fail, and they will subsequently have to resort to employing a parry).

★

Progression 1 (Attack and Counter-Attack)
Fencer A: step with engagement on Fencer B's sixte and disengage lunge on Fencer B's pressure.
Fencer B: return pressure on Fencer A's engagement, circular parry of sixte and riposte direct or by disengage.

Progression 2
Fencer A: step with engagement in sixte and disengage-counter-disengage compound attack with lunge on Fencer B's pressure.
Fencer B: return pressure on Fencer A's engagement, circular parry of sixte (fails).

Progression 3
Fencer A: step with engagement in sixte and disengage-counter-disengage compound attack with lunge on Fencer B's pressure.
Fencer B: return pressure on Fencer A's engagement and then counter-attack with a thrust in octave.

Progression 4
Fencer A: step with engagement in sixte and, on Fencer B's pressure, disengage lunge to the upper target with lunge or flèche.
Fencer B: return pressure on Fencer A's engagement and then thrust with the blade in octave (this will fail and Fencer B will subsequently have to resort to employing a parry).

*

Progression 1 (Riposte and Remise)
[here is diagram 5 placed to the right of and aligned with the text]
Fencer A: from Fencer B's engagement in sixte, disengage lunge.
Fencer B: parry quarte and riposte direct to score.

Riposte

Progression 2
Fencer A: from Fencer B's engagement in sixte, disengage lunge as a false attack.
Fencer B: parry quarte and riposte direct.
Fencer A: parry quarte and counter-riposte by disengage (second intention).

Counter Riposte

Progression 3
Fencer A: from Fencer B's engagement in sixte, disengage lunge.
Fencer B: parry quarte and compound riposte by one-two to score.
Fencer A: attempt to parry Fencer B's compound riposte.

Compound Riposte

Progression 4
Fencer A: from Fencer B's engagement in sixte, disengage lunge and pause for a remise (second intention).
Fencer B: parry quarte and compound riposte by one-two.
Fencer A: immediately recover from the remise and parry Fencer B's riposte.

Remise

Progression 5
Fencer A: from Fencer B's engagement in sixte, disengage lunge and pause for a remise.
Fencer B: parry quarte and riposte direct to score (Fencer A's remise will be out of time and he or she will have to employ a counter-riposte).

Riposte

*

Progression 1 (Riposte and Remise)
Fencer A: on Fencer B's engagement in quarte, cut-over lunge.
Fencer B: parry high sixte and riposte to chest with a step forward.

Progression 2
Fencer A: on Fencer B's engagement in quarte, cut-over lunge as a false attack.
Fencer B: parry high sixte and riposte to chest with a step forward.
Fencer A: recover with parry in seconde and riposte by detachment to shoulder (second intention).

Progression 3
Fencer A: on Fencer B's engagement in quarte, cut-over lunge as a false attack.
Fencer B: parry high sixte and compound riposte with a feint low, disengage high, stepping forward and evading Fencer A's seconde parry.

Progression 4
Fencer A: on Fencer B's engagement in quarte, cut-over lunge as a false attack and pause for a remise.
Fencer B: parry high sixte and compound riposte, stepping forward.
Fencer A: place the remise and recover to close the line in sixte.

Inducing the Attack

In 'Defence: Parries – Reaction, Premeditation and Inducement' it was seen that an inducement by way of a feint-parry could be offered to draw an attack into a known final line in order to score with a premeditated parry and riposte. The success of such a stroke is often because the opponent, as aggressor and having started the action, on seeing the defender's response, instinctively believes that, as attacker, they also have the initiative and are therefore fully committed to the final attack.

Consider for a moment an aggressive attacker, having prepared with one or more blade actions, advancing quickly with a feint and launching the final phase of a compound attack. The momentary sight of the defender's parry (or feint-parry!) confirms the attacker's resolve beyond the point of no return. Likewise, a similarly aggressive attacker, seeing the opponent's blade lifting in line for a stop-hit, will be committed to the final delivery of a direct attack. Therefore it is not only the use of a feint-parry that can be used to induce and defeat an attack; a feint of stop-hit may also be employed.

In 'Defence: Counter-Offensive Actions' in Part 4 we saw the difficulties and dangers of employing counter-offensive actions. We also saw that the counter-attack can be exploited by the simple attack. In fact, many fencers at intermediate level and above are very aware of the failings of spontaneous stop-hits and are tactically adept at exploiting them. Preceded by a speedy preparation, they commence an action of attack that is slow, and/ or wide, and/or extending progressively and then complete the attack as the defender extends for a stop-hit.

In other words, the final resolve of the simple attack is as much dependent on the brief sighting of a counter-attack as the compound attack is dependent on the sighting of a parry. Therefore a feint of stop-hit at the appropriate moment can be used to trigger the final delivery of the attack, which in turn can be parried and a riposte delivered.

We should also realise that simply waiting passively for the final delivery of the attack in order to parry is insufficient. If the attacker fails to see any response at the moment of moving from preparation to offence and just before the moment of total commitment, he or she may abort the attack for fear of the waiting defence. Many fencers have highly trained automated responses and only the stimulus of the parry or stop-hit will ensure their final delivery (unless they have managed to close the distance so that they are within the defender's reaction time, and there is no impediment to delivering the hit). The feint of stop-hit should be formed at the crucial moment when the attacker moves from preparation to attack, and the parry is formed with a step back.

Training Game Exercises

In both exercises each progression needs to be repeated several times before moving on. The two game objectives are: (1) for Fencer B to recognise and exploit stop-hits that are 'out of time' and (2) for Fencer A to develop the use and control of feint stop-hits and feint-parries.

Progression 1
Fencer B: step with quarte engagement and detachment, lunge with slow but progressive extension.
Fencer A: parry and riposte.
Fencer B: *either* permit the riposte to land *or* attempt to deceive the parry.

Progression 2
Fencer B: step with quarte engagement and detachment. Lunge with slow but progressive extension.
Fencer A: stop-hit *or* parry and riposte *or* remain passive.
Fencer B: if the stop-hit is perceived, complete the attack. If the parry is perceived take a first counter-riposte, but if Fencer A remains passive abort the attack.

Progression 3
Fencer B: step with quarte engagement and detachment. Lunge with slow but progressive extension.
Fencer A: *either* stop-hit *or* parry and riposte *or* feint of stop-hit and parry riposte.
Fencer B: if the stop-hit is perceived, complete the attack. If the parry is perceived, take a first counter-riposte.

★

Progression 1

Fencer B: advance with a double engagement quarte-sixte, followed by a disengage feint.

Fencer A: return pressure and then either parry or extend for a stop-hit.

Fencer B: either deceive the parry or deliver the original feint as a direct attack.

Progression 2

Fencer B: advance with a double engagement quarte-sixte, followed by a disengage feint.

Fencer A: return pressure and then either parry or extend for a stop-hit. Sometimes attempt feint-parry followed by parry and riposte of Fencer B's attack.

Progression 3

Fencer B: advance with a double engagement quarte-sixte, followed by a disengage feint.

Fencer A: return pressure and then either parry or extend for a stop-hit. Sometimes attempt feint stop-hit followed by parry and riposte of Fencer B's attack.

The Winning Hit

The technical elements of fencing covered in this book include the fundamental positions and movements, the actions of preparation, offence, counter-offence, defence and renewal, and the use of simple, compound and broken-time actions. The tactical material covered demonstrates the relationship between technical elements and how they may be exploited, one to defeat the other.

There is no masterstroke, no master tactic. Fencing is a game of speed, action, reaction and strategy in which the winning stroke is the one correctly employed *at the appropriate moment.* Such a winning stroke, although unique to that moment, is also the culmination of the practice of all the technical and tactical content of fencing that has gone before.

A truly competent fencer is one who has the repertoire of all the technical actions in the hand and tactical knowledge in the head, and the ability to use both. That ability must also include the capability to react not only appropriately, but also promptly. Therefore the fencer needs to drill both the mechanical and responsive actions of the bout extensively and repeatedly in order for those actions to be reproduced within a tactical framework at precisely the right moment; this is 'timing' or 'tempo'.

However, success is not only a combination of the appropriate moments both mechanically and tactically, but also opportunistically. To interpret timing simply on the basis of mechanical action is not enough. As I have already said, to be successful, a hit needs to be delivered at the precise moment that the opponent is incapable, hesitant or distracted; when they are preoccupied and unready; or when they have lost the initiative. This latter sense of timing only develops with experience but the newer competitive fencer should observe potential opponents to discover such moments, no matter how fleeting. They should also use practice bouts not only for technical and tactical practice, but also to familiarise themselves with opportunistic moments.

In seeking to attack with tempo, observe the opponent's preparations, feints and attacks, and then, in anticipation of their action, attack at the moment when they are least able to deal with it. This moment is usually as they commence or are just recovering from an action as follows:

1) the opponent's preparation – attack the commencement or the recovery.
2) the opponent's feint – attack the commencement or the recovery.
3) the opponent's attack – attack on the opponent's recovery.
4) the opponent's hesitation – attack immediately.

A hit delivered confidently and with perfect timing will not only score a point, but will also, at the very least, annoy the opponent, and at best it will devastate their confidence.

In the Introduction I made the point that the three T's, Technique, Tactics and Timing, are the passport of today's fencer; perhaps we can add to that a T for Tenacity, as learning to fence well is no short-term project, and progressing to competitive success can take years of dedication with little reward other than that glorious release and exhilaration when you score the last hit of the last fight. That sensation and memory will surpass even the presentation of the medal or cup that results from it.

The material that I have provided in this book will, I hope, help you on a journey to that experience, be it in school, club or competition; or simply to enjoy the pleasure of physical and intellectual success as a leisure fencer.

I have covered a broad range of strokes and tactics in this volume and not all suit everyone. Some strokes are more frequent in use than others, although they occupy the same space in this book. Some actions, like every other aspect of life, are subject to changes of fashion. Take what you will and mould it to suit your game – fencing.

Appendix A

The Conventions of Fencing

Always remember that fencing rewards the player who takes the initiative; the fencer who is physically and intellectually ahead in the game gains the victory. In foil fencing the fencer who initiates an attack has priority over any action made by the opponent in response. If such a response is offensive it is termed a 'counter-offensive'. The convention requires that a fencer who is subjected to an attack should first successfully deflect or otherwise avoid the opponent's blade before taking an offensive action in turn. Similarly, that action must be deflected if a fencer is to regain priority. If two fencers both hit, then only the one with the right of way will score. However, if only one fencer hits, then clearly that fencer scores. When both fencers are judged to have simultaneously conceived and executed successful attacks then neither fencer scores as neither has priority.

Some common fencing conventions are discussed below.

Right of Way

This is a common term used to explain the priority of an action when both fencers are hit. So, a point in line has priority or right of way over an attack, and an attack has right of way over the counter-attack. Similarly a simple riposte has right of way over a remise.

Fencing Time

This is defined as the time taken to execute a blade or foot movement and is one concept used by a referee in deciding the priority of a hit. It follows that overcomplex, extraneous, or unnecessary actions of blade or foot may cause the fencer to be vulnerable in that he or she inadvertently delays the delivery of their hit and is attacked during their preparation. Likewise, an overly delayed riposte or counter-riposte would be defeated by a renewed action from the opponent if that renewed action struck before the commencement of the final action of the riposte.

Point in Line and Dérobement

A fencer who stands with their arm extended and point threatening the target has right of way over a fencer who rests on guard. Should the fencer who is on guard launch an offensive and fall onto the point without first deflecting it, then he or she is counted as hit because this is the fencer who has committed a 'suicidal' error. Likewise, if both fencers are standing with point in line and one should lunge, then the priority remains with the line. It is necessary to avoid or deflect the point in line in order to take the initiative and score.

Neither fencer may commence (or recommence) a bout with the point in line, but must start or resume a bout from on guard.

The Attack

An attack is defined as the first offensive action whereby the weapon is advancing towards and threatening the opponent's target. This is not to say that the blade has to be in line with the target (a common misconception) but that it is moving towards the target in a continuous, unbroken movement from the point where its movement commenced.

Sometimes it is difficult to decide which fencer is the attacker, and often both fencers consider themselves due a point and the opponent to be 'out of time'. An eager fencer will view the concept of attack and counter-attack much as a tennis player views a line call – they see what they desire to see, and therefore the adjudication of the referee is absolute!

Parry and Riposte

In recognition of the dominant and advantageous position of the defender following the successful parry of an attack (or other offensive action), the defender has the right to retaliate (riposte). A simple riposte executed without delay will always have priority over a subsequent action by the original attacker – even if, in actual time, it arrives fractionally after the attacker's second action!

The Conventions of Fencing

Beats and Engagements

A beat or engagement in itself has no priority or right of way. However, an attack launched by engaging or beating the opposing blade, and then immediately extending towards the opponent will be seen clearly by a referee as having priority over any offensive action launched into it. More clearly in fact than an attack launched maintaining absence of blades. Also, a beat lunge against a point in line will have priority if the fencer in line simply seeks to re-establish that line.

Counter-Attacks

A counter-attack is one launched into the opponent's attack. If the attack is avoided (either through body evasion or opposition of the blade) then clearly, if successful, the counter-attack scores. Otherwise it must arrive at least one period of fencing time ahead of the attack to be valid.

Compound Attacks

A correctly executed compound attack (i.e., an attack with one or more feints of the blade) is intended to evade a parry or parries. However, some compound attacks are poorly executed, thus provoking or panicking the opponent to thrust into them. In this case the referee must decided whether (a) the fencer executing the compound action was clearly hit before they began the delivery of their offensive action (in which case it is judged that they have been attacked on their preparation); (b) the fencer executing the compound action was hit during a feint preceding the commencement of the final action (in which case the counter-attack is in time); or (c) the fencer executing the compound action was hit only during or after the delivery of their final offensive action (in which case they are judged to have right of way as the attacker, and the opponent's action is out of time as a counter-attack).

Appendix B

Footwork Development

The advance, retire and the half-step have already been introduced. They are not natural actions and their unusual locomotion is only acquired by constant practice in the early days. However, gone are the times when some fencing masters could insist that their pupils be drilled in footwork exercises for months before touching a weapon. The glamour of the blade is the attraction for the tyro fencer of today, and the necessary footwork skills have to be developed alongside weapon skills.

Each training or fencing session should ideally begin with a general physical warm-up into which some specific fencing actions can be incorporated (see the 'Footwork during the Warm-up' section further on). This warm-up can then be followed by a period of footwork training prior to the group or individual lessons and training bouts. Such footwork training can be in the form of drills, pairs exercises or games, and a selection of such exercises follows.

Training and practice exercises that require a long sequence of steps forward should be avoided. In game-like practices, haste takes over from controlled movement and the technical quality of the footwork can deteriorate. Further, a long series of steps is not realistic to the bout because the fencer should have decided on or reacted with an action within the first step or two – any later means that he or she is advancing without an objective.

The following drills are to assist in the development of mobility and balance. When practising foot actions, place the hands on the hips or let them hang loosely from on guard, and always maintain a minimum distance of two foot-lengths between the feet.

Exercises

1) Simultaneously raise and lower the heel of your rear foot and the toes of your front foot. Maintain bent knees and do not allow your hips to rise.
Repeat twice followed by a step forward (the step forward finishes with the same coordination of heel and toe), then step back. Repeat as two small rapid steps and a third step (maintain the heel and toe coordination), then step back.

1a) Simultaneously raise and lower the heel of your rear foot and the toes of your front foot, then the heel of your front foot and the toes of your rear foot in succession (treading).

2) Extend the front foot so that the heel touches the ground 20 cm ahead and return to guard. Maintain a bent rear knee without any rise or fall in the hips, and keep your body weight divided equally between both feet. Repeat twice, and then complete a step forward before stepping back with two steps.

3) Reach back 20–30 cm with the rear foot. Keep the front foot in place but raise the toe. Return to guard. Do not permit your body weight to move over the rear foot. Repeat twice and then complete a step back before advancing.

3a) Reach back 20–30 cm with the rear foot. Return to guard and lunge or step-lunge.

4) Combine drills 2) and 3). Extend the front foot to touch the ground with the heel, return and step forward. Reach back with the rear foot, return and step back. The objective is to maintain the balance and posture of the on-guard position and to avoid shifting the body weight onto either the front or rear foot at any time.

5) Extend the front foot so that the heel touches the ground 20 cm ahead and return to guard. Extend the front foot so that the heel touches the ground again, then advance the foot a further

10 cm before completing the step. Follow with a short step forward or back.

6) Extend the front foot so that the heel touches the ground 20 cm ahead, then advance the heel a further 10 cm to briefly touch the ground again. Complete a lunge. The rear leg thrusts on the final phase of the foot exercise. The objective is to maintain balance throughout the lunge, prevent the weight shifting forward early or over the front leg and thereby shortening the lunge, and to control the timing of the thrust from the rear leg.

Pair Work Without Weapons

7) Two fencers stand 10–20 cm outside lunging distance. The lead fencer may advance or retire no more than one or two steps or half-steps at a time. The following fencer tries to maintain the distance. The objective is for the lead fencer to draw the other into or inside fencing distance. At the instant of success the lead fencer claps and the fencers change roles.

8) From outside lunging distance and stepping on the spot, the lead fencer advances one foot and the other fencer remains static; however, if the other fencer steps back, then the lead fencer lengthens the step forward with the front heel momentarily touching the ground in mid-step.

8a) As above but concluding with a flèche.

9) One fencer is on guard and stepping on the spot. The partner stands a little ahead and to one side. The partner presents the hand at chest height as a target. Using a lunge, the fencer must touch hand to hand. Occasionally the partner increases the distance of the hand, but only after the fencer has commenced the lunge (and well before it is completed). The fencer aborts the original lunge by landing the front foot and so completes a step before lunging, thus reacting to cover the greater distance.

9a) As above but the action is completed by aborting the lunge, landing the front foot and flèching.

10) Two fencers stand 10–20 cm outside lunging distance. The lead fencer may advance one or two steps before lunging, recovering and retiring. On the recovery the following fencer executes a lunge or step-lunge according to whether the attack was delivered with one step or two. The objective is to control the delivery of an attack on the opponent's recovery.

11) As above but the lead fencer sometimes recovers with an extended arm. The objective for the lead fencer is to tempt the other fencer to advance precipitately, and for the following fencer to avoid such a situation. Practise later with weapon in hand.

12) As above but, from time to time, the fencer pauses in the lunge, again to exploit a fencer who advances too early. The objective for the following fencer is, once more, to avoid such a situation. Practise later with weapon in hand.

13) From stepping on the spot, the leading fencer steps forward or back and slightly to the left or right of the fencing line. The objective is for the following fencer to maintain both the distance and the fencing line.

13a) The leading fencer advances and retires at will, occasionally with a step forward slightly to the left or right of the fencing line. The objective is for the following fencer to maintain both the distance and the fencing line.

14) The fencer stands on guard and the partner stands off to one side holding a glove along the fencing line at full arm extension from the fencer. When the fencer claps, the partner releases the glove. The fencer extends to catch the glove before it falls.

14a) As above but at an increased distance and performed with a half-step on the extension.

14b) As 14) or 14a) but, having caught the glove, carry it forward in a lunge or flèche.

15) The leading fencer advances and retires at will. The partner touches the hand of the leading fencer and retires rapidly. The lead fencer attempts to touch with a step-lunge only.

15a) As above but the fencers start from stepping on the spot.

More Footwork

In addition to the step or half-step, the fencers can incorporate jumps (balestras) to introduce attacks, and cross-over steps for advancing and retiring. The jump can be either a short dramatic action or a longer smoother movement. In either case, as with a step forward, the front foot precedes the rear foot when starting. The difference is in the completion of the action as both feet land at the same time, flat and without the cadence of the heel-toe action of the front foot. A feint or beat can be employed simultaneously with the landing of the jump to provoke a response to be exploited. For a direct attack with a beat, the beat may be timed very slightly ahead of the landing, so that the blade rebounds towards the target and is delivered by a lunge that rebounds from the jump and is given greater speed. To practise the jump, swing the front foot forward, take a short hop forward with the rear foot, and land on guard.

16) Jump forward, half-step and recover, followed by jump, half-step lunge and recover, followed by jump, half-step and flèche.

17) Jump forward, half-step and recover, followed by jump, step and lunge. Vary the step between a small rapid step and a step with a change of cadence (slowing with the front foot action and accelerating towards the end of the step).

18) Step forward, jump, half-step and either recover or flèche.

The crossover is also used to close or open distance. In advancing, the rear foot moves first and is passed ahead of the front foot before that too is brought forward to re-establish the normal stance. In retiring, the front foot leads and passes behind the rear foot. The fencing line is maintained throughout.

The crossover can be preceded by a half-step of the front foot, or completed with a half-step of the rear foot.

Footwork During the Warm-up

Some sports specific footwork and allied fencing actions can be included in the general warm-up that precedes a training session.

1) Whilst jogging, intersperse with two or three fencing footsteps, sometimes leading with the left foot and sometimes with the right.

2) Whilst jogging, on a given signal (clap), jump/land on guard, pause and flèche, then resume jogging.

3) On a given signal, land on guard. Bring the heels closer together with a small jump, touch both hands on the ground between the feet and return to on guard.

4) As 3) but touch the ground with the rear hand only, whilst thrusting the sword hand at head height (duck stop-hit).

5) As 3) but from touching the ground, jump into the lunge position (spring lunge).

6) From jogging, on a given signal, jump into on guard, touch the floor in front of the leading foot, then flèche to resume jogging.

7) From jogging, on a given signal, jump into on guard and take two steps back. On a second signal, jump, on guard, through 180 degrees and resume jogging.

Lunge Exercises

1) Start in the lunge position. Recover to on guard and lunge again. Recover to on guard and flèche.

2) Start in the lunge position. Recover to on guard and lunge again. Start the recovery, but lunge again before the front foot completes the recovery.

3) From on guard, jump into the lunge, recover (backwards) and flèche.

4) Start in the lunge position, tap the rear foot then the front foot on the floor. Repeat, followed by a flèche.

5) Start in the lunge position, tap the front foot then the rear foot on the floor. Repeat, followed by a flèche.

6) Start in the lunge position, tap the rear foot then the front foot on the floor. Tap the rear foot on the floor to launch a short reprise by lunge.

Group Footwork and Games

1) The group mirrors the actions of the coach or leader whilst maintaining distance. The coach, on guard, steps forward and backwards, and employs half-steps. When the coach's hand is lowered the group should extend their sword arms; when the coach's arm is lowered again, the group should lunge, and as the coach's arm is raised the group then returns to guard from the lunge.

Variations

- add cross-overs
- add flèche when the coach claps
- add duck stop-hit when the coach lunges
- add step-lunge on the coach's recovery from the lunge (but not if the arm remains extended)

2) The group advances and retires at random. On one clap from the coach the arm is extended, on two claps the arm is extended and followed by a lunge and recovery to guard.

3) The coach calls a short series of 'one' or 'two'. On 'one' the group takes a smaller step than normal, on 'two' a normal step.

Variations

- the coach adds one or two claps for extension or extension and lunge
- as above, but the direction changes after each lunge
- the direction changes with each new set of numbers

4) The group are in pairs in two rows, facing each other and on guard, at closer than fencing distance and stepping on the spot. When the coach says 'salt' row A advances and row B retires, but when the coach says 'sugar', row B advances and row A retires. The objective is for the fencers to respond correctly and maintain a safe distance. Additionally, if their partner makes an error and inadvertently comes too close then the facing fencer attempts to touch or catch their hand.

Variations

- occasionally intersperse other commands (e.g. 'sock') which the fencers should ignore
- increase the distance and use a lunge (instead of a step) to catch the opponent's hand
- at the increased distance not only should the attacker lunge, but the defender should also attempt to attack with a step-lunge on the original attacker's recovery

5) The group are in pairs in two facing rows at fencing distance and stepping on the spot. The coach gives one, two or three claps. On one clap, row A steps forward and back. On two claps they extend the arm, step forward and back. On three claps they extend and lunge or step-lunge. Row B must try to maintain a safe distance.

Footwork, Distance and Bladework Combined

The following pairs exercises (with weapons) are designed to improve the fencer's ability to quickly adapt or change the footwork to changes of distance and bladework.

Fencer A: engage quarte with a half-step.

Fencer B: *either* circular change of engagement in place *or* retire and take circular change of engagement followed by lateral parry.

Fencer A: counter-disengage flèche from half-step *or* complete the step with a counter-disengage feint followed by a disengage lunge or flèche.

★

Fencer B: engage blade in sixte or quarte with half-step forward.

Fencer A: circular change of engagement and light graze forward.

Fencer B: *either* lateral parry in place *or* recover with two lateral parries.

Fencer A: disengage attack with a medium-length lunge *or* attack by one-two with a fully extended lunge.

★

Fencer A: step forward with a double engagement of quarte-sixte.

Fencer B: *either* take a circular change of engagement in place *or* step back with a circular change of engagement followed by a lateral parry.

Fencer A: counter-disengage lunge (or flèche) *or* step with a counter-disengagement and feint followed by a disengagement and lunge.

★

Fencer A: step with a beat feint direct, counter-disengagement, followed by a second counter-disengagement (doublé) and lunge.

Fencer B: *either* take two circular parries in place *or* step back before taking the circular parries.

Fencer A: if Fencer B steps back, pause the blade in the feint whilst taking a further step, and then lunge with the doublé. Alternatively a half-step and flèche may be used to deliver the doublé.

★

Fencer A: step forward with quarte, counter-quarte engagement and lunge direct.

Fencer B: *either* evade the quarte engagement in place *or* step back with the evasion followed by a simple parry if a feint is perceived.

Fencer A: if Fencer B steps back, abort the intended lunge and step with a feint direct before deceiving the parry and lunging.

★

Fencer A: jump, half-step and pause.

Fencer B: engage quarte *or* extend the blade in line from sixte.

Fencer A: disengage feint whilst advancing the rear foot and complete a one-two lunge or beat and direct attack against the line.

Appendix C

Glossary of Fencing Terms

The following terms are given in English and French. The translation of some terms from Italian or Hungarian, for example, may use the same vocabulary but convey a different meaning. As the rules of the international governing body, the Fédération Internationale d'Escrime (F.I.E), are in French, it is the French terminology and sense that is used here.

A

À propos: see *timing*.

Absence du fer: see *absence of blades*.

Absence of blades: when the adversaries' blades are not in contact.

Actions contre-offensives: see *counter-attack*.

Actions simultanées: see *simultaneous attacks*.

Aides/Aids: the last three fingers of the sword hand that assist in the manipulation of the handle.

Angulation: the inclination of the blade and sword hand from the arm in order to strike at an oblique target.

Appel: a foot action of striking the ground with the sole of the front foot to distract the opponent.

Appuntata (It): a remise into a delayed riposte.

Arbitre: a judge, see also *referee*.

Arrêt: see *stop-hit*.

Arrêt avec fer: see *time-hit*.

Assaut: see *bout*.

Assesseur: a judge, see *referee*.

Attack: the initial offensive action in a phrase, initiated with a progressive movement of hand and blade towards the target. It may be simple or compound.

Attack on the blade: an action, such as a beat, against the opponent's blade.

Attaque: see *attack*.

Attaque au fer: see *attack on the blade*.

Attaque composée: see *compound attack*.

Attaque progressive: see *progressive attack*.

Attaque renouvelée: see *renewed attack*.

Attaque simple: see *simple attack*.

B

Balestra: a jump-like advance when both feet land simultaneously.

Barrage: a fight off; when two fencers of the same ranking must fight for promotion.

Battement: see *beat*.

Bind: a prise de fer that transports the opposing blade diagonally.

Beat: the action of striking the opponent's blade with one's own.

Beat parry: a parry that is formed by striking the attacking blade rather than maintaining opposition.

Blade in line: an extension of arm and blade from shoulder to point threatening the opponent; in foil and sabre the blade in line has priority over an attack.

Bout: the combat between two fencers.

Broken time: an attack or riposte that pauses in its delivery in order to exploit the rhythm of the opponent's defence.

C

Ceding parry: a parry formed by yielding to the pressure of a prise de fer attack.

Change beat: beating the blade on the opposite side to that which was originally engaged.

Change coulé: a coulé formed on the opposite side to that which was originally engaged.

Changement d'engagement: see *change of engagement*.

Change froissement: a froissement formed on the blade on the opposite side to that which was originally engaged.

Change of engagement: re-engagement of the blade on the opposite side to that which was originally engaged.

Change of intention: an attack that is spontaneously modified because of an unexpected response. See also *choice reaction*.

Change pressure: a pressure formed on the blade on the opposite side to that which was originally engaged.

Changez-battez: see *change beat*.

Changez-coulez: see *change coulé*.

Changez-froissez: see *change froissement*.

Changez-pressez: see *change pressure*.

Choice of action: a fencing drill where the fencer has free choice of two or more strokes in a phrase, usually the initial or final action.

Choice reaction: a fencing drill where two or more conclusions are possible. See also *open-eyes attack* and *change of intention*.

Cible: target.

Circular parry: a parry that forms a circle, starting and finishing in the same line.

Closed distance: close quarters, a distance at which the arm needs to be bent and/or an angulation formed in order to hit.

Composite attack: see *compound attack*.

Compound attack: an attack with one or more feints.

Compound preparation: see *preparation*.

Compound counter-riposte: a counter-riposte with one or more feints.

Compound riposte: a riposte with one or more feints.

Continuation: general term for a renewed offensive action (for example, redouble of attack or riposte).

Contre-attaque: see *counter-attack*.

Contre-dégagement: see *counter-disengage*.

Contre-parade: see *circular parry*.

Contre-riposte: see *counter-riposte*.

Contre-temps: see *counter-time*.

Copertino (It): a change of pressure as an attack.

Coquille: the shell or guard of the weapon.

Corps à corps: body contact between two fencers. This will automatically stop the bout, as fencing is a non-contact sport.

Coulé: see *graze*.

Counter-attack: an offensive action into an attack; see *stop-hit* and *time-hit*.

Counter-disengagement: an evasive action that avoids a circular engagement.

Counter-offensive: see *counter-attack*.

Counter-parry: see *circular-parry*.

Counter-riposte: the offensive action taken following the parry of a riposte (or counter-riposte); it may be immediate, delayed, simple or compound, with or without prise de fer or broken time. If immediate and simple it will have priority over any renewal of the riposte.

Counter-time: an offensive action that responds to the opponent's counter-attack; usually an act of second intention whereby the counter-attack is parried in order to deliver a riposte.

Coup d'arrêt: see *stop-hit*.

Coup de temps: see *time-hit*.

Coup double: see *double-hit*.

Coup droit: direct attack.

Coup (déjà) lancé: a hit in the course of delivery when a fight is halted – valid except on the expiry of time.

Coup lancé: see *thrown-hit*.

Couper la ligne: see *cutting the line*.

Coupé: see *cut-over*.

Couvert: see *covered*.

Covered: a position of engagement where the opponent cannot score by direct thrust.

Croisé: a prise de fer whereby the opposing blade is taken from high to low (or vice versa) on the same side.

Crosse: orthopaedic grip. See *poignée*.

Cut-over: an evasion of the opponent's blade made by passing over the point as opposed to using a disengagement or counter-disengagement.

Cutting the line: a semicircular parry that moves from high to low (or vice versa) and simultaneously from inside to outside (or vice versa). Sometimes referred to as a diagonal parry.

D

Dégagement: disengagement.

Demi-cercle: a semicircular parry from sixte to high septime.

Dérobement: an evasive action against the opponent's attempt to engage, beat or take the blade which is in line with the point threatening the target.

Destructive parry: the parry from quarte to septime that intercepts the attacking disengagement and so acts both as parry and prise de fer. With a slight forward thrust it is capable of disarming the opponent.

Deuxième intention: see *second intention*.

Development: the successive and coordinated progression of the weapon and limbs when forming a lunge.

Diagonal parry: see *cutting the line*.

Direct attack: a simple attack without evasion of the opponent's blade.

Directeur du combat: see *referee*.

Disengagement: an evasion of the opponent's attempt to engage or the release therefrom. See also *counter-disengagement*.

Distance: the distance between two fencers in order that the target may be hit. This may also be classified as riposting distance (where only the extension of the arm is necessary) or lunging distance. The distance for the commencement of a bout is 4 metres.

Doigté: see *fingerplay*.

Double engagement: a succession of engagement and change of engagement by the same fencer.

Double hit: where two fencers are judged to have hit at the same time but one has priority over the other (for example, an attack and counter-attack) as opposed to simultaneous attacks.

Double parry: a succession of two parries to deflect an attack (or riposte) and its renewal. See also *successive parries*.

Double preparation: see *preparation*.

Doublement: a compound offensive action of disengage feint followed by counter-disengagement.

Doublé: a compound offensive action composed of a counter-disengage feint followed by trompement of counter-disengagement.

E

En garde: on guard.

En marchant: see *progressive attack*.

Engagement: contact with the opposing blade. The engagement may be a light contact or hold the opposing blade covered in one of the lines or guards, for example, sixte.

Enveloppement: a circular prise de fer.

F

Faible: see *foible*.

False attack: an attack not intended to hit but to explore or exploit the opponent's response.

Feint: a threat with the blade to provoke a response that is then exploited, either by the use of a compound action, a counter-riposte or by counter-time.

Feint-parry: a partly formed parry intended to trigger the opponent's attack.

Fencing distance: see *distance*.

Fencing line: an imaginary line that joins the heels and front toes of two fencers.

Fencing measure: the distance of a lunge separating two fencers. See *distance*.

Fencing time: the duration of a single action of blade and/or foot; a convention that assists in prioritising actions in a bout.

Filo (It): see *graze*.

Fingerplay: the use of the fingers (the manipulators and aids) by relaxation and contraction to control the handle of the weapon.

First counter-riposte: the reply made by the original attacker on the opponent's riposte; it may be by reaction or as second intention.

First intention: an attack delivered without thought of a subsequent stroke or tactic.

Flancon(n)ade: a prise de fer through quarte and quinte to strike at the flank.

Flèche: 'arrow', an attack delivered with advancement of the sword arm and body accompanied by propulsion from the front leg but without advancement of the front foot.

Flick hit: a misnomer. See *thrown hit*.

Foible: the part of the blade nearest the point.

Forcer: to engage with force.

Fort(e): the part of the blade nearest the guard.

Froissement: an attack on the blade with pressure combined with a vigorous grazing action from the foible to the middle of the opposing blade.

G

Garde: see *guard*.

Graze: an action along the blade to prepare or launch an attack.

Guard: (i) the protective shell of the weapon (ii) a protective stance, for example, guard of sixte.

H

Half parry: see *feint-parry*.

Half-step: an incomplete step forward or backward.

High line(s): see *line*.

High septime: the blade position with the hand raised in septime that protects from hits arriving over the blade. Used to lift thrusts safely past the position of septime.

High sixte (or neuvième): the blade position with the hand raised in sixte that protects from hits arriving over the blade.

I

Indirect attack: a simple attack that is not direct, for example, delivered by disengage, counter-disengage or cut-over.

Indirect riposte: a simple riposte that is not direct, for example, delivered by disengage, counter-disengage or cut-over.

In quartata (It): a counter-attack along the line of quarte with body displacement.

Insufficient parry: a parry which, although making contact, fails to sufficiently cover the line being protected and fails to deflect the attacking blade from the target.

Invito: 'invitation', the deliberate opening of a line offering the possibility of attack to the opponent.

L

Lame: blade.

Lamé: see *plastron*.

Liement: see *bind*.

Ligne d'engagement: see *fencing line*.

Line(s): (i) see *blade in line* (ii) high lines – blade positions of sixte and quarte and the imaginary lines from them (iii) low lines – blade positions of septime and octave and the imaginary lines from them (iv) high lines – blade positions of sixte and quarte and the targets protected by them (v) low lines – blade positions of septime and octave and the targets protected by them. Low line(s): see *line*.

M

Manipulators: the thumb and forefinger which are primarily responsible for the control and direction of the weapon. See *aids*.

Mesure d'escrime: see *fencing measure*.

Mezzocerchio (It): half-circle parry lifting to high sixte.

Muette: see *silent lesson*.

N

Neuvième: the ninth position of the blade. See *prime*; otherwise known as high sixte.

O

Octave: the eighth position of the blade. See *prime*.

One-two: a compound attack consisting of a disengage feint followed by a trompement by disengagement.

Open-eyes attack: an attack that commences without premeditation of the opponent's response and adapts accordingly as opposed to 'change of intention' where the fencer reacts when a preconceived response does not materialise. See *choice reaction*.

Opposition: a thrust that maintains contact with the opposing blade and so covers the attacker's target in the line of thrust.

Opposition parry: a parry that maintains contact with the blade during (and after) the formation of the parry.

P

Parade: see *parry*.

Parade circulaire: see *circular parry*.

Parade composée: see *successive parries*.

Parade en cédant: see *ceding parry*.

Parade de contraction: a parry that intercepts the final deception of a compound attack.

Parade direct: lateral parry.

Parade d'opposition: see *opposition parry*.

Parade du tac: see *beat parry*.

Parade insuffisante: see *insufficient parry*.

Parade latérale: lateral parry.

Parade semicirculaire: see *semicircular parry*.

Parades successives: see *successive parries*.

Parry: a defensive action with the blade; it may be simple (lateral), circular or semicircular; it may have a beat-like quality or maintain opposition. See *principle of defence*.

Passata sotto (It): historic counter-attack, ducking whilst lunging back.

Phrase: the sequence of offensive exchanges between two fencers.

Pied ferme: see *progressive attack*.

Piste: 'strip', the area of play for a bout.

Plastron: (i) protective vest worn under the jacket of a fencer for added protection to the armpit (ii) pad worn by a fencing coach for protection of the body (iii) plastron métallique; a metallic vest worn over the fencing jacket to record hits at foil and sabre.

Poignée: handle or grip. See *crosse*.

Pommel: the weighted base of the handle which also serves to dis/assemble the weapon.

Première intention: see *first intention*.

Preparation: an action of blade, foot, or body, preparatory to an attack (but not part of the attack); it may be compound (two actions performed at the same time; for example, a step with an engagement) or double (two actions performed in succession).

President: see *referee*.

Pression: see *pressure*.

Pressure: preparation or commencement of an attack by applying leverage to the opponent's blade in the same line as contact.

Prime: the first position of the blade. Historically the position obtained by drawing a weapon from its scabbard.

Priority: the convention (at foil and sabre) that recognises that one action has advantage over another even though both actions may hit. The line has priority over an attack.

Principle of defence: the opposition of the forte of the defending blade to the foible of the opposing blade in order to deflect a thrust.

Prise de fer: an action that levers and controls the opponent's blade either combined with the attack or as a preparation for attack. See *bind*, *croisé* and *envelopment*.

Progressive attack: a compound attack performed with the feint and deception formed whilst lunging as opposed to advancing (en marchant) or fixed footed (pied ferme).

Pronation: hand position whereby the palm faces downwards (for example, seconde). See *supination*.

Q

Quarte: the fourth position of the blade. See *prime*.

Quinte: the fifth position of the blade. See *prime*; with foil and épée it is a further rotation from quarte, with sabre it protects the head; both positions are pronated.

R

Rassemblement: the bringing of the feet together, usually by withdrawing the front foot to the rear whilst performing a stop-hit.

Redouble: a renewal of attack or riposte in a new line (for example, by disengage or cut-over), the first having been parried (usually an opposition parry). Performed at riposting distance in the lunge or during the recovery.

Referee: formerly President, also Directeur du Combat; assisted by judges.

Remise: a renewal of attack or riposte in the same line, the first having been parried (usually the parry has been followed by a detachment). Performed at riposting distance in the lunge or during the recovery; usually an act of second intention.

Renewed attack: a further attack following the failure of the first; see *remise*, *reprise* and *redouble*.

Replacement: a misnomer – see *remise* and *redouble*.

Reprise: the renewal of attack or riposte (the first having been parried) and requiring a further forward action by lunge or flèche. The blade action may be simple or compound, with or without an attack on the blade.

Right of way: see *priority*.

Riposte: the offensive action taken following the parry of an attack; it may be immediate, delayed, simple or compound, with or without prise de fer or broken time; if immediate and simple it will have priority over any renewal of the attack.

Riposte composée: see *compound riposte*.

Riposting distance: see *distance*.

Rompre: to retire; step back.

S

Salut(e): the courtesy of acknowledging the opponent (and referee) at the commencement and conclusion of a bout, usually by raising the weapon to the mask.

Salute des armes: a choreographed sequence of guards and thrusts to introduce a display of fencing.

Sauter: a fencer who lunges by lifting the front foot in an arc rather than extending in a line.

Second(e) intention: a tactic where the first offensive is a ploy in order to launch a premeditated second offensive exploiting the opponent's response (for example, first counter-riposte, counter-time, remise).

Seconde: the second position of the blade. See *prime*.

Semicircular parry: a parry formed with such an action, for example, from sixte to octave.

Semi-supination: see *supination*.

Sentiment du fer: the feel of the blade through the fingers permitting interpretation of the opponent's position and action.

Septime: the seventh position of the blade. See *prime*.

Silent lesson: a lesson or drill without verbal command; the pupil responds only to the blade.

Simple attack: an attack without a feint; it may be direct or indirect and is executed in one period of time coordinated with a step, lunge or flèche.

Simultaneous attacks: when the opponents conceive and execute attacks at the same moment.

Sixte: the sixth position of the blade; the classic fencing guard for the commencement of a bout. See *prime*.

Stop-hit: a counter-attack into the opponent's feint or attack. To be valid it must arrive before the commencement of the attacker's final action.

Successive parries: two or more parries to deflect a compound attack (or riposte).

Supination: hand position whereby the palm faces upwards (for example, sixte). In modern fencing the palm is more likely to be in a vertical plane.

T

Temps d'escrime: see *fencing time*.

Temps perdu: see *broken time*.

Through beat: a grazing beat that strikes and passes over the point of the blade.

Thrown hit: a hit delivered in cut-over-like fashion exploiting the momentum gained from the weighted point of a modern foil or épée; also called coup lancé.

Tierce: the third position of the blade. See *prime*.

Time-hit: an old term having the concept of a stop-hit with opposition so that the final thrust of the attack is intercepted.

Timing: the moment suitable for launching an offence to immediately exploit an action of the opponent.

Trompement: an extended and threatening blade to deceive the opponent's attempt to parry (as in a dérobement or the final action of a compound attack).

U

Under plastron: see *plastron*.

Un-deux: see *one-two*.